chocolate
cakes

chocolate cakes

50 great cakes for every occasion

BY ELINOR KLIVANS

Photographs by Ann Stratton

CHRONICLE BOOKS

SAN FRANCISCO

dedication

It is always for Jeff.

Remembering my mom—we baked, we laughed, and we made cakes and memories.

Library of Congress Cataloging-in-Publication Data available.

ISBN 978-0-8118-6872-3

Manufactured in China

Design by Anne Donnard
Prop styling by Bette Blau
Food styling by Liz Duffy
Typesetting by DC Typography, San Francisco
The photographer wishes to thank her entire team that worked on this incredibly yummy project, especially Bette Blau for her endless enthusiasm and her beautiful props and Liz Duffy for her creativity and hard work. She would also like to thank her assistants Danelle Manthey who could not have been more attentive to the smallest details and Tanya Salazar for keeping her on track in this digital age. A big thank you to all!

10 9 8 7 6 5 4 3 2 1

Chronicle Books LLC
680 Second Street
San Francisco, California 94107
www.chroniclebooks.com

acknowledgments

Judith Weber, my friend and my agent, who watches over me and my work.

Bill LeBlond, my editorial director, and Amy Treadwell and Sarah Billingsley, my editors, who make my books happen in the best possible way.

Ann Stratton, the photographer, Liz Duffy and Bette Blau, prop stylists who made and photographed my cakes in a way that made me want to make every one all over again.

A giant thank-you to Doug Ogan, Anne Donnard, Tera Killip, Peter Perez, and David Hawk, the brilliant publishing team at Chronicle Books.

Judith Dunham, my copyeditor, who also loved this book and helped make it better.

My family, Laura and Michael Williams and Kate Steinheimer and Peter Klivans; they bake, they taste, they support, they care.

My grandchildren, Charlie, Madison, Max, Sadie, Kip, and Oliver, who think their grandmother makes good cakes and who love to help her bake, decorate, and lick the spoons.

My father, who is proud of me and loves my books.

Thank you to the chocolate-cake testers who tested so many recipes so carefully: Jennifer Goldsmith, Katherine Henry, Cheryl Matevish, Melissa McDaniel, Rachel Ossakow, Dawn Ryan, Allyson Shames, Louise Shames, Kate Steinheimer, Laura Williams, and Charlie Williams.

A big thank-you to my circle of supporters and encouragers: Melanie Barnard, Flo Braker, Sue Chase, Rosalee and Chris Glass, Michael Drons, Susan Dunning, Maureen Egan, Carole and Woody Emanuel, Karen and Michael Good, Kat and Howard Grossman, Faith and David Hague, Helen and Reg Hall, Carolyn and Ted Hoffman, Kristine Kidd, Alice and Norman Klivans, Susan Lasky, Robert Laurence, Rosie Levitan, Gordon Paine, Joan and Graham Phaup, Janet and Alan Roberts, Pam and Stephen Ross, Louise and Erv Shames, Barbara and Max Steinheimer, Kathy Stiefel, Elaine and Wil Wolfson, and Jeffrey Young.

contents

a quartet of quick-start recipes   22

chocolate cakes for a quick chocolate fix   32

big one-layer chocolate cakes   50

chocolate layer cakes 80

party chocolate cakes 112

introduction

As I got to the end of testing recipes for this book, I was buried in chocolate cakes. My freezer was full. I had marched cakes up to the neighbors, served them to company, carried them on airplanes to family and friends, and brought them everywhere that I had been invited to for months. I sent out this e-mail to my friends:

Dear Friends,

I have too many chocolate cakes! So, I have decided to have a chocolate cake party.

I hope you all can come next Friday, September 5, at 7:30 p.m., to help me out and have a good chocolate time. House guests are welcome.

The replies were enthusiastic: "Wonderful idea!" "What a great idea! We are so glad to help you out with your chocolate cake dilemma." "Yummy! We will be there!"

That same spirit continued right through the party as we feasted for hours on chocolate cake. When I looked at the table of cakes I had produced, even I was surprised at the variety. I had ice cream cakes, multilayer cakes, cupcakes, pudding cakes, big tube cakes, meringue cakes, cake rolls, deep-dish cakes, chiffon cakes, cheesecakes. It was the happiest party I had ever given— I knew chocolate cake would do that. It always does.

chocolate grows on trees

I haven't found a place yet where the proverbial money grows on trees, but I found the next best thing that does—chocolate. About ten years ago, I had an opportunity to see the process of making chocolate, from harvesting the cocoa beans in a jungle plantation to manufacturing chocolate in a factory.

Out of the blue, a Venezuelan chocolate manufacturer called to invite me to travel with a small group to his country. We would visit the jungle where the cacao trees grow, then fly to the factory where the beans are turned into chocolate. This was extremely unusual because, after cocoa beans are dried, they are normally shipped to chocolate manufacturers around the world for processing. A trip like this was an opportunity that happens rarely to food writers—at least to this one.

Four of us arrived in Caracas, where we boarded a small plane. Next, we traveled by four-wheel-drive vehicle over paved roads, then dirt roads, and then a dirt track, which led to the cocoa plantation. We walked through rows of cacao trees protected from the sun by the shade of tall, leafy trees. Although the cacao trees require a hot climate, they must be shaded from direct sunlight. I was surrounded by a jungle of chocolate. Granted, it was chocolate in its raw, unprocessed, cocoa pod state, but it was still a forest of chocolate-to-be.

Cacao trees require a hot tropical climate with abundant rainfall and thrive within 10 degrees latitude of the equator. Possessing these conditions, Venezuela has a long history of cocoa farming, as do other South American countries and various countries in Central America and Africa.

The cocoa pods themselves look downright comical, as they grow right out of the trunk or branch of the cacao tree. They resemble small elongated pumpkins that someone has glued to the trees. Although October to January and April to May are the peak harvest months, cocoa pods can be harvested year-round. The same tree at the same time of year can have cocoa blossom flowers and cocoa pods in all the shades of green, yellow, orange, and brown, the sequence that they go through to reach maturity.

The harvesting is a hands-on operation. After the cocoa pods are cut from the trees, they are brought to a central location on the plantation. One man quickly chops the end from each pod with a whack of his machete. He throws the open pods to workers nearby, who use a type of wooden spoon to scoop out the cocoa beans along with the sticky white pulp that surrounds them. One worker with a machete can keep four men busy scooping. The empty pods are thrown into a huge pile. They will be composted and later used to fertilize the cacao trees. Bees buzz around the sweet, sticky, pulp-covered beans. There is a sweet odor in the air, but not a hint of chocolate.

The beans are transferred indoors to bins to ferment for several days. The air in the fermenting rooms is thick and smells like that in a winery, but does not have the aroma of chocolate. During this process, the sticky white pulp dissolves, and the cocoa beans begin developing more complex flavors.

After fermenting, the beans are spread out on a large wooden platform to dry. If it rains, the entire platform can be rolled under cover to keep the beans dry. When dry, the beans look like large, elongated, dark brown coffee beans. Now they give off a faint odor of chocolate. After being sized and graded, the beans are shipped from the plantation to factories for processing into dark chocolate, milk chocolate, white chocolate, and cocoa powder.

Returning to Caracas, we went to the chocolate factory. There, the beans are cleaned to remove dirt, and any inferior beans are discarded. Next the beans are roasted, and at last the aroma of chocolate fills the air. Roasting cocoa beans is a carefully controlled process, during which many chemical changes take place that determine the final flavor of the chocolate. Once the beans are roasted, the shell is easy to crack, and the nibs or kernels can be removed. The shells are sent off to be used for fertilizer, garden mulch, or animal food; the nibs are processed into chocolate.

Traditionally, factories blended nibs from different plantations and cocoa bean varieties to produce various chocolate flavors. Recently, however, single-origin chocolates have become popular. Some chocolates are made from beans grown in the same region or even the same plantation.

Just more than half of the cocoa nibs are cocoa butter, and just under half are dry cocoa mass or cocoa solids. Finely grinding the nibs between large rollers produces chocolate liquor. The resulting chocolate liquor, consisting of both cocoa butter and cocoa mass, is a dark brown paste that cools and hardens into unsweetened chocolate. This is the chocolate base from which all kinds of chocolate are manufactured. When some of the cocoa butter is pressed out of chocolate liquor, cocoa powder is left. Blending additional cocoa butter and sugar with chocolate liquor produces eating chocolate. The amount of added sugar and cocoa butter controls the sweetness and texture of the chocolate from semisweet (plain) to bittersweet. Milk chocolate contains powdered or condensed milk along with cocoa butter and sugar. White chocolate contains only cocoa butter, plus milk solids, sugar, and other flavorings.

The chocolate is further refined between giant steel rollers. Refining grinds the chocolate and sugar into tiny particles and produces a smooth, silken texture. Fine chocolate then goes through a conching process, whereby it is kneaded and constantly stirred in giant vats. Watching this process and smelling the chocolate make for a pure chocolate experience. Conching, by further reducing the size of the particles and rounding off their edges, gives the chocolate an ultrasmooth texture. During conching, more cocoa butter, emulsifiers, and flavorings may be added. The liquid chocolate is carefully cooled at a controlled temperature that tempers it and prevents the cocoa butter from forming grainy crystals. Finally, the chocolate is molded into many forms: large blocks for commercial use, small blocks for candy bars, and specialized bars and squares for baking. Happily, our tour ended with several hours of chocolate tasting.

all about chocolate cake

Here are the basic guidelines for making good chocolate cakes. I begin with the chocolate. Without question, using good-quality chocolate is essential for making a good chocolate cake. Then you need to gather the other ingredients and, in some cases, ready them, such as toasting nuts. Tips for choosing pans and other necessary equipment and for mixing cakes will help you achieve a successful outcome. Finally, it is time to bake the cakes and store them.

choosing, melting, and storing chocolate

Basic to making a good-tasting chocolate cake is to use good chocolate. As with all baking ingredients, you do not need to choose the cheapest or necessarily the most expensive chocolate, but you want to seek out the best quality. Supermarkets now offer a broad selection, including semisweet (plain), milk, white, and especially bittersweet chocolate. My superscientific method is to taste the chocolate—a fun job in itself. Try two or three different brands at a time, and keep to the same type for each tasting—all semisweet or all milk. As you sample the chocolate, let it melt in your mouth and decide if it has a pleasant chocolate flavor and leaves an aftertaste of chocolate rather than sugar or chemicals. You will also notice that different brands have different flavor nuances. You can choose the one that appeals to your personal taste. The bottom line is that if chocolate tastes good by itself, it will taste good in your cakes.

Many brands of bittersweet chocolate state the percentage of cacao. Bittersweet chocolate that contains beween 60 and 70 percent cacao is a good choice. When selecting white chocolate, check that the packaging lists cocoa butter as one of the ingredients. When cocoa powder is treated with an alkaline solution, it is called Dutch-process cocoa powder. I prefer Dutch-process cocoa powder because it has a slightly sweeter flavor and darker color than nonalkalized cocoa powder.

Think low and slow when melting chocolate. A piece of chocolate in your mouth is melting at your body temperature, which averages 98.6°F (37°C). You could hold the chocolate in your mouth for a long time (if you had that much willpower), and it would never burn or turn grainy. That is because it is melting slowly at a consistent low temperature. Use this example as your guide when you melt chocolate for baking: melt it slowly over gentle heat, without subjecting it to sudden temperature changes. Exposure to high heat or to a burst of steam from boiling water burns chocolate, just as it would burn your hand. At high temperatures, chocolate also can become lumpy and grainy. If you want to be exacting, you can measure the temperature with an instant-read thermometer. Chocolate begins to melt at 92°F (33°C) and should be completely melted at 113°F (45°C). Just remember low and slow.

Before melting chocolate, use a large, sharp knife to chop it into ½-in (12-mm) pieces so it will melt evenly. Large pieces could become too warm on the outside before the inside has a chance to melt. Put the chopped chocolate—or the chocolate plus other ingredients that must be melted with it—in a heatproof bowl and set the bowl on top of a pan of barely simmering (not boiling) water. You can also use a double boiler.

Keep in mind that the bottom of the bowl, or the top pan of the double boiler, should not touch the hot water. Stirring will help the chocolate melt evenly. As soon as it melts, remove the bowl from the pan of hot water. To melt chocolate in a microwave, follow the manufacturer's directions.

All chocolates are best stored in a cool, dry place. If handled properly, unsweetened, semisweet (plain), and bitter-sweet chocolate will keep for up to one year. Since milk chocolate and white chocolate contain milk solids, they are more perishable than dark chocolate. I store milk chocolate for up to three months. White chocolate, lacking chocolate liquor, is more perishable than other chocolates. If I am storing it for more than three weeks, I wrap it tightly in plastic wrap and then in heavy aluminum foil, and keep it in the freezer. White chocolate should be defrosted in its wrapping so that any condensation will form on the wrapper and not on the chocolate. I store unsweetened cocoa powder for up to two years in a tightly covered tin in a cool, dark place.

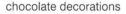

chocolate decorations

Decorations can be as simple as grating chocolate over a cake or as fancy as covering the top of a cake with curled shavings of chocolate. Whether simple or fancy, none of these decorations is difficult to make—even though they might look that way. Some of the following decorations are used for the cakes in this book. Others can be added to these or any other cakes that you bake.

Chocolate decorations can be made from bittersweet, semisweet (plain), milk, or white chocolate. A mix of dark and white chocolate decorations often looks attractive. Unsweetened chocolate tastes too bitter to use for edible decorations. Chocolate decorations melt easily when handled with warm hands. Instead, use a spoon or spatula to lift them and arrange them on a cake. Because decorations are less likely to break if used cold or frozen, it is a good idea to chill or freeze them before use or, better yet, to make them ahead and store them in the freezer for up to three months.

Begin by melting the chocolate (see page 12).

making chocolate lace. Line a baking sheet (tray) with parchment (baking) paper. Use a teaspoon to drizzle thin lines of dark, milk, or white chocolate, or a combination, over the paper, working in a circular motion to make a lace pattern or crisscrossing the lines to form a crosshatch pattern. Make sure that the lines connect so that the pattern has a sturdy structure. Three oz (85 g) of chocolate will cover an area about 12 by 10 in (30.5 by 25 cm). For a pleasing color contrast, drizzle lines of white chocolate over lines of dark chocolate or dark over white. Put the baking sheet in the freezer for about 30 minutes to firm the chocolate. Carefully turn over the paper on the baking sheet and peel the paper from the chocolate. Break or cut the frozen chocolate into randomly shaped pieces 3 to 5 in (7.5 to 12 cm) in size to decorate a whipped cream–topped cake such as Mocha Whipped Cream Truffle Cake (page 85). Turn the chocolate lace top up to use it.

making chocolate shards, cutouts, and other shapes. Chocolate triangles, strips, squares, and rectangles of any size are cut with a knife; circles, leaves, hearts, half-moons, and stars are cut with metal cookie cutters of different sizes.

To make chocolate shards, turn a rimmed baking sheet (tray) upside down, cover it with parchment (baking) paper, and tape the paper to the sheet with masking tape. The baking sheet supports the paper and chocolate, and the tape keeps the paper from sliding when you spread the melted chocolate. Use a thin metal spatula to spread about 6 oz (170 g) of melted chocolate evenly over the paper into a rectangle about

9 by 12 in (23 by 30 cm). Or, use more chocolate for a larger rectangle, or less for a smaller one. The chocolate should be thick enough so that the paper does not show through. At this stage, the chocolate looks shiny and wet. Chill the chocolate-covered sheet in the refrigerator until the chocolate hardens, about 30 minutes. Break the chocolate into random-size pieces and use it to decorate cakes. Try stacking shards on top of a cake or pressing them onto the sides of frosted cakes.

To make cutout shapes, follow the instructions for preparing the baking sheet (tray) and spreading the chocolate into a 9-by-12-in (23-by-30-cm) rectangle. Chill the chocolate just until it looks dull and dry, and is still soft but no longer melted. This will take about 3 minutes for dark chocolate and about 5 minutes for white chocolate. Do not let the chocolate harden, as it tends to shatter when cut or pressed with a metal cutter. The chocolate can also sit at room temperature until it looks dull and dry and is firm enough so that the edges do not run together when the chocolate is cut. Depending on the room temperature, this can take from 10 minutes to 1 hour. Use a metal cutter to cut out star, heart, leaf, or other shapes. The Chocolate Yule Log (page 134), for example, is decorated with chocolate leaf cutouts. Press the cutter firmly to cut cleanly and completely through the chocolate. Depending on the size of the cutter, you will have twelve to twenty-four shapes. Return the

cut chocolate to the refrigerator to firm completely, about 30 minutes or up to overnight. Remove the baking sheet from the refrigerator. Carefully turn the chocolate-covered paper on the sheet and peel the paper from the chocolate. The cutouts will separate from the chocolate rectangle. If any shapes do not release easily, use a small, sharp knife to separate them from the chocolate.

To make squares, triangles, and strips, follow the instructions for preparing the baking sheet (tray) and spreading the chocolate into a 9-by-12-in (23-by-30-cm) rectangle. Chill the chocolate as directed for making cutouts. Use a large, sharp knife to trim the edges of the rectangle, if necessary, so it is precisely 9 by 12 inches. Then use a small, smooth-bladed (not serrated) knife to mark twelve 3-in (7.5-cm) squares, or any shape desired, on the chocolate. Cut each square diagonally into triangles, if you like. Or, cut the squares into short, narrow strips, like those used for the Chinese Five-Spice Chocolate Chiffon Cake (page 59). Do not draw the knife across the chocolate; instead, press down to make clean, sharp edges. The knife should cut completely through the chocolate, and the chocolate should be firm enough so that it does not cling to the knife. If the chocolate is too soft and runs together, chill it for 1 or 2 minutes, watching it carefully, or let it sit at room temperature until it is firm enough to hold the cut marks. If the chocolate hardens and then cracks when it is cut, warm the chocolate sheet in a low oven, about 200°F (93°C), for a few seconds. It is preferable not to chill or rewarm the chocolate repeatedly so it retains its even color.

making chocolate shavings and curls. A stainless-steel vegetable peeler with a swivel blade is a good tool for making curls. The only tricks to making the curls are to use a large, thick piece of chocolate—about 8 oz (225 g) is a good size— and to have the chocolate in a very slightly softened state. To check the temperature, try making a few curls. If the chocolate is too firm, flakes form. If the chocolate is too soft, soft lumps clog the vegetable peeler. When the chocolate is at the right temperature, curls roll easily off the vegetable peeler. White and milk chocolate are softer than dark choco-late, and on a warm day they may be ready to form curls without any preparation.

Have ready a baking sheet (tray) lined with parchment (baking) paper. Warm the chocolate between the palms of your hands for about 2 minutes. White and milk chocolate take less time to soften; any chocolate takes longer to warm up if the room is cold. When the chocolate is ready, it will feel slightly sticky. In this state, dark chocolate loses some of its shine. Another method is to put the chocolate in a sunny window for about 5 minutes, being sure to watch it closely so it doesn't melt.

Hold the block of chocolate in one hand. Moving the vegetable peeler away from you, scrape curls from the block in a single layer, using long strokes of 1½ to 2 in (4 to 5 cm) and forming curls about 1 in (2.5 cm) wide. Let the curls fall gently onto the lined baking sheet, using a small spoon to gently separate any that touch. Scrape along all sides of the chocolate block. The curls will vary in shape and size; longer curls will roll over themselves, and shorter shavings will have a curved shape. If the chocolate begins to flake and break rather than form curls, it is too hard and should be held between your hands again or put in the sun until it softens. If the chocolate is too soft and starts to clog the vegetable peeler, let it sit at room temperature or chill it briefly until it is firm enough. When the block of chocolate becomes too small to form curls, save it for another use. You can make about 4 cups of chocolate curls from an 8-oz (225-g) block of chocolate.

Put the baking sheet with the chocolate curls in the freezer for about 30 minutes to firm them. Use a spoon to place them carefully over the top of a dessert or to press them gently onto the sides of a frosted cake. You can also place the curls in a tightly sealed container and freeze them for up to 1 month. Chocolate curls look best on a dessert when placed in a thick, generous layer.

adding color to white chocolate. White chocolate and food coloring are all you need to make colored chocolate. I prefer soft pastels; for stronger colors, add more food coloring. Begin with 2 oz (55 g) of melted white chocolate in a small bowl. Squeeze a drop of food coloring onto a plate, dip the tip of a knife into the coloring, and stir it into the chocolate. Repeat the process until you have the desired color. Adding coloring sparingly gives you control over the results. For the Deep-Dish White Chocolate Peaches-and-Cream Cake (page 107), I fol-lowed this method and used yellow and red food coloring to produce the soft peach color in a small quantity of melted white chocolate. Then I swirled this peach-colored white chocolate into the larger quantity of melted white chocolate. Colored chocolate can also be drizzled onto any dark or white chocolate shape or decoration.

other ingredients

butter and oil

I use unsalted butter so I can control the quantity of salt added to baked goods. For recipes that require oil for the shortening, I choose canola or corn oil.

cake syrups

Applied to cake layers with a pastry brush, syrups add flavor and moistness to cakes. They also help frosting adhere. These quick-to-prepare syrups are made from sugar dissolved in hot water and flavorings that match or enhance the cake. Liqueurs and coffee are common flavorings.

citrus zest

Zest is the outside colored part of the rind of lemons, limes, and oranges. Rinse fruit with warm water and dry it before grating the zest. Be careful to grate only the colored part of citrus rind; the white pith under the rind is bitter. An average lemon or lime yields 2 to 3 tbsp juice and 2 tsp zest. A medium orange yields about ¼ cup (60 ml) juice and 2 to 3 tsp zest. Generally, the firmer the fruit, the less juice it will yield.

cream

The heavy (double) cream in this book's recipes, also sometimes called heavy whipping cream, contains 36 to 40 percent butterfat. Heavy cream has more butterfat, whips firmer, and holds up longer than cream labeled whipping cream.

eggs

For consistent results, I use large eggs. Cold eggs will separate more easily than room-temperature ones.

flavorings and spices

Choose pure vanilla extract (essence), made from vanilla beans, and pure almond extract (essence), which contains oil of bitter almond. You can check spices by tasting a tiny bit to make sure they are fresh. Store spices tightly covered and replace stale ones. Storage times vary, but are measured in months, not years. I use kosher salt, which is free of preservatives. Although slightly coarse, it passes through my flour sifter and strainer.

flour

The recipes call for either unbleached all-purpose (plain) flour or cake (soft-wheat) flour. Cake flour is fine textured and is used to make an especially light cake. Be sure to sift flour when a recipe calls for sifting. Sifting removes large particles, distributes leavenings and other dry ingredients evenly, and makes a difference in the texture of the final cake.

leavening agents

Baking soda (bicarbonate of soda) is an alkaline leavening that is combined with an acid ingredient such as buttermilk, sour cream, or molasses to activate it. When mixed into a moist batter, the baking soda is activated and the batter should be baked promptly. If kept dry, baking soda can be stored indefinitely.

I use double-acting baking powder. It contains baking soda, which is alkaline, and two acid ingredients, one activated by liquid and the other by heat. Store baking powder tightly covered, and do not use it past the expiration date that is usually printed on the bottom of the can.

nuts

When new crops of nuts appear in markets, I replenish my supply, seal the nuts tightly in a freezer bag or plastic freezer container, and store them for up to one year. It is easy to remove just what I need for a recipe. Nuts should be defrosted before using so that they do not turn batters cold and thick.

Toasting intensifies the flavor of nuts such as walnuts and pecans. In the case of almonds and hazelnuts (filberts), toasting actually changes their taste. If nuts are frozen, thaw them before toasting or allow additional baking time.

To toast nuts, spread them in a single layer on a rimmed baking sheet (tray) and preheat the oven. Toast walnuts and pecans at 325°F (165°C/gas mark 3) for 8 to 10 minutes; sliced (flaked) or slivered almonds at 350°F (180°C/gas mark 4) for 12 to 15 minutes; and whole almonds and hazelnuts at 350°F (180°C/gas mark 4) for 15 to 20 minutes. Shake the sheet once to redistribute the nuts and ensure that they toast evenly, and watch them carefully to prevent them from burning. Just before the nuts are ready, you should smell a pleasant aroma. Hazelnuts (filberts) acquire a sheen from the oil that rises to their surface during baking.

Hazelnuts must have their bitter skins removed before toasting. Peeled hazelnuts are usually available in specialty markets. Otherwise, I find blanching is the easiest way to remove the skins. To blanch the nuts, bring a saucepan of water to a boil. Add the hazelnuts and boil, uncovered, for 5 minutes. Drain the hazelnuts, immerse them in cold water for several minutes, drain them again, and peel the nuts with a small, sharp knife. The skins will come off easily, and the nuts will dry out in the oven when they are toasted. If the hazelnuts are not toasted immediately, dry them with a kitchen towel and refrigerate or freeze them.

Nuts can be chopped in a food processor, but I prefer to chop them with a large, sharp knife, which allows more control of the resulting texture. A food processor invariably grinds some of the nuts, which won't ruin a recipe but might change it slightly. When a recipe calls for finely chopped nuts, they are about 1/8 in (3 mm); coarsely chopped nuts are 1/4 to 3/8 in (6 mm to 1 cm). To grind rather than chop nuts, a food processor fitted with the steel blade works well. For finely ground nuts, process the nuts with some of the sugar or flour used in the recipe, which allows the nuts to become finely ground without forming a paste.

sugars and sweeteners

Store all sugars in a tightly covered container to keep them dry and free from insects. Brown sugar will become hard if not kept tightly sealed. Brown sugar contains molasses, and dark brown sugar has a larger quantity of molasses and adds a darker color to baked goods. Corn syup and molasses should be stored in the refrigerator to prevent mold. I use unsulphured molasses, which has not been processed with sulphur and has a milder flavor than sulphured molasses.

equipment

baking pans

Cakes should be baked in good-quality heavyweight pans. Shiny baking pans that reflect heat are less likely to produce overbaked cake bottoms than dark-colored baking pans, which absorb heat.

It is important to use pans of the right size. If the recipe calls for cake layers baked in a 9-in (23-cm) round pan, and an 8-in (20-cm) pan is used instead, the result can be quite different—and not for the better. The height of the pan's sides is also important. Pans that are at least 1¾ in (4.5 cm) high will prevent cakes from spilling over the rim as the batter rises. Pans are measured from the inside. To determine the capacity, put the pan on a level surface and add water, 1 cup (240 ml) at a time.

Lining pans with parchment (baking) paper ensures that cakes will release easily from the pans. The practice also facilitates cleanup.

electric mixers

Beating is easy with an electric mixer, and even an inexpensive handheld mixer will work fine for the recipes in this book. The mixer I use is a 5-qt (4.8-L) KitchenAid stand mixer, which has a bowl large enough to hold the batter for any of my cake recipes. Attachments include a flat beater for beating batters and a whisk for beating egg whites and whipping cream.

miscellaneous utensils

Graters are handy for grating citrus rind. A Microplane grater or a four-sided box grater works well. Have on hand several sets of measuring spoons, a set of dry measuring cups, and a liquid measuring cup. A rolling pin is useful for crushing cookies into crumbs. Rubber, or preferably silicone, spatulas in several sizes are ideal for folding light and heavy mixtures together and for scraping the last bit of batter or frosting from a bowl. A fine-mesh strainer can do double duty: to strain mixtures and to sift flour. For a regular flour sifter, I prefer one with a rotary handle. A stainless-steel sauce whisk is invaluable for whisking a mixture until smooth and for blending melted chocolate with whipped cream or other ingredients.

ovens

No matter how well an oven is calibrated, its temperature is sometimes inaccurate or can vary. For example, I have a new, properly calibrated oven, but I notice that when I open the oven door to put in a cake, the temperature can quickly drop. The oven temperature also rises and falls during baking until the thermostat kicks in to adjust the temperature to the preset level. These factors make it necessary to check a cake as it bakes, especially as the end of the baking time nears.

I tested the cakes in this book in a conventional electric oven, but they can be baked in a convection oven, which has a fan that circulates the hot air. If you are using a convection oven, the temperature needs to be modified; check the manufacturer's guidelines to determine temperature and baking time adjustments. Throughout my baking life, I have owned several brands of convection ovens and found they all had different requirements.

wire racks

Most cakes are removed from their pans and cooled on wire racks. The air circulation enables cakes to cool evenly. It is useful to have two racks. Some cakes cool in their pans, but on wire racks for more even cooling and air circulation.

mixing cakes

At the beginning of each recipe, you will find the baking time and oven temperature, and the time needed to mix a cake and any filling or frosting. The mixing time assumes that the ingredients are gathered and ready to go. When you make a recipe for the first time, you will probably need more than the stated time. Being familiar with a recipe makes it come together faster.

Most of the batters for the cake recipes are mixed by one of three methods. Batters made with softened butter, such as Devil's Food Cake (page 28), are mixed by creaming butter and sugar and then beating in the eggs. The flour and liquid, if any, are added at the end in alternate portions. Thorough beating is important to develop the cake's structure when creaming the butter and sugar and when adding the eggs. When the dry ingredients and liquid are added, they are mixed only until blended, rather than requiring long beating.

White Chocolate Cake (page 30) is an example of light-textured butter cake layers mixed by beating eggs and sugar to a thick, fluffy mass, then mixing in flour, warm milk, and melted butter. The structure of the cake develops from the thorough beating of the eggs and sugar. The warm milk mixture helps stabilize the beaten eggs. It would be very difficult to overbeat the egg and sugar mixture, so if you are in doubt about whether the mixture is sufficiently beaten, you can continue beating for another minute or two. The purpose of the remainder of the mixing process is just to incorporate the ingredients smoothly. The batter is thin and bakes into a fine-grained cake.

For cakes that use oil as the shortening, such as the Chocolate-Hazelnut Sour Cream Cake (page 61), the light structure of the cake develops during a thorough beating of the eggs with the sugar. Once this fluffy mixture is achieved, the remainder of the mixing process involves blending the ingredients together to incorporate them into the batter.

Meringue cakes and chiffon cakes depend on properly beaten egg whites for their light, fluffy texture. The beaten whites should be shiny and form a soft point or peak when you dip a spoon in the whites and lift it out. When beaten whites are at this soft peak stage, the movement of the beaters will form smooth, curving lines in the whites.

To beat egg whites, start with the mixer on low speed. Place the eggs in a bowl. Add the cream of tartar, which helps stabilize the whites, and beat until it is dissolved. Increase the speed to medium and continue beating until soft peaks form. It is easier to control the results on medium speed than on high speed. Sugar stabilizes the egg white foam, and once the sugar is added, the mixture, or meringue, thickens. Add the sugar slowly so the egg whites have time to absorb it; sprinkle in 1 or 2 tbsp every 15 to 30 seconds. Continue beating until the whites form stiff peaks, or as directed in a recipe.

When combining a lighter mixture with a heavier mixture or combining warm melted chocolate with cold whipped cream, you want to end up with a smooth result without deflating your carefully beaten or whipped mixture. First, use a whisk or rubber spatula to lighten the heavier mixture by stirring in a small amount of the lighter mixture until smoothly combined. Whisking whipped cream into melted chocolate creates a smooth chocolate base that is light enough for the remaining whipped cream to be folded into it. Following this method helps keep any hard bits of cooled chocolate from forming as you fold the two mixtures together. Finally, use the rubber spatula to fold the remaining light mixture into the heavier one. Bring the edge of the spatula down to the bottom of the bowl and then lift the two mixtures up and over each other, turning the bowl as you fold, until they are smoothly blended.

baking

The question that I am asked most often about baking is "How do I know when something is done?" Since ovens do not bake in the same way, baking times are approximate. When the end of the baking time nears—5 to 8 minutes before the recommended time—begin checking the cake.

Each recipe gives at least one visual test: lightly touching the top of the cake for firmness, checking the color, seeing if the cake is pulling away from the sides of the pan, or testing the cake with a toothpick. If you insert the toothpick into the edge of a cake, and then into the center, you will be able to feel the difference between a still-liquid center and a baked edge. Meringues are done when they feel crisp on the outside.

Leaving a baked cake in the pan for 10 to 15 minutes gives it time to settle and firm slightly. This also makes the cake easy to remove from the pan. Exceptions are Chinese Five-Spice Chocolate Chiffon Cake (page 59), which cools in the pan, and Pear and Chocolate Crumb Cake (page 71), which is cut and served from the pan. I invert cake layers onto a wire rack to cool and, in most cases, leave the firmer top of the cake down. Placing the paper liner from the pan over the cake while it cools prevents the cake from drying out.

You may seldom think about the temperature in your kitchen, but if you ever watch ice cream melt quickly on the kitchen counter on a hot summer day or cream cheese take hours to soften in a cold kitchen, you will realize that the room temperature can affect mixing and baking cakes. Batters may need to bake for a longer or shorter time if they are mixed in a cold or warm kitchen. In a warm kitchen, chocolate melts fast and butter softens quickly; cream should be whipped quickly while still cold. In a cold kitchen, on the other hand, you might have to allow more time for butter and cream cheese to soften.

storing and freezing cakes

Generally, desserts served at room temperature are stored at room temperature, and those served cold are stored in the refrigerator. A frosted chocolate cake or a chocolate cheesecake stored in the refrigerator should sit at room temperature for about 15 minutes before serving, to soften the frosting or filling and bring out the flavors.

To protect a cake decorated with soft frostings or topped with whipped cream, insert several toothpicks in the top and cover the cake carefully with plastic wrap (cling film). The toothpicks keep the plastic from compressing the topping. The tiny holes in the cake will not be noticeable when the toothpicks are removed.

Cakes without frosting, cakes with rich chocolate or cream cheese frostings and fillings, and cakes with chocolate glazes freeze well for up to one month. Cakes with whipped cream toppings and fillings or those with fresh fruit do not freeze well. To freeze a cake, cool it thoroughly. Wrap an unfrosted cake in plastic wrap and then in heavy aluminum foil. If the cake has frosting, freeze it, without wrapping it, to firm the frosting or glaze, and then wrap it in plastic wrap and heavy aluminum foil. Label the cake with the name and the date. Defrost cakes without unwrapping them so that condensation forms on the foil rather than on the cake.

Many cakes without frosting can be sent to friends and family. If you are willing to give up the pan (a nice gift, too), it makes a great container for shipping. Wrap the cooled cake in its pan with plastic wrap (cling film) and heavy aluminum foil. Then enclose the cake in bubble wrap and pack it in a carton. If you are shipping a cake without the pan, tape cardboard to the top and bottom of the wrapped cake. Then surround the cake with bubble wrap and pack it in a carton. Fill the carton with packing material so that the cake fits securely. Be sure to ship by the fastest, most economically feasible method.

a quartet of quick-start recipes

Simple Chocolate Buttercream 25 ✳ Ganache and Whipped Ganache 26

Devil's Food Cake 28 ✳ White Chocolate Cake 30

Here are a frosting, a glaze or filling, and two cakes that recur in very different guises throughout the book. These are also the recipes I make time and time again. I often bake a cake one day and add the filling and frosting a day later. The baked cake cools overnight and is easy to handle the next day, and finishing the cake takes just minutes.

With these four recipes—a creamy frosting, a fudgy or creamy ganache, a chocolate cake, and a white chocolate cake—you can create many different combinations. The cake recipes give options for making two 9-in (23-cm) layers, one 10-in (25-cm) layer, or one 9-in square. It is handy to know that 9-in round cakes can also be baked in 8-in (20-cm) square pans, and a 10-in round cake can be baked in a 9-in square pan. By adding flavorings, a white chocolate layer can become a lemon, orange, or cinnamon cake, for example. Similarly, a chocolate glaze or a chocolate buttercream can be flavored with spices, liqueurs, orange zest, or coffee.

You can bake these cake layers ahead and freeze them (see page 20). Cold cake layers are easier to handle than room-temperature or freshly baked ones. When filling and frosting frozen layers, defrost them just to the point that they can be cut easily. They are sturdy and will not crumble or break.

simple chocolate buttercream

MAKES 4 CUPS (960 ML)

This creamy, dark chocolate frosting is cause for applause when spread on any cake, but slathered on chocolate cake layers or chocolate cupcakes, or rolled up in a cake layer, it will surely generate a standing ovation. When freshly made, the buttercream has the creamiest texture and spreads easily. Be sure to clean the icing spatula on the edge of the bowl each time you spread the frosting; this keeps cake crumbs from sticking to it.

☀ Mixing time 5 minutes

3	OZ (85 G) UNSWEETENED CHOCOLATE, CHOPPED
4	OZ (115 G) SEMISWEET (PLAIN) CHOCOLATE, CHOPPED
⅓	CUP (75 ML) HEAVY (DOUBLE) CREAM, AT ROOM TEMPERATURE
1	TSP INSTANT COFFEE GRANULES
¾	CUP (170 G) UNSALTED BUTTER, AT ROOM TEMPERATURE
2½	CUPS (250 G) POWDERED (ICING) SUGAR
⅛	TSP SALT
1	TSP VANILLA EXTRACT (ESSENCE)

Put both chocolates in a heatproof bowl (or the top of a double boiler) and place it over, but not touching, barely simmering water in a saucepan (or the bottom of the double boiler). Stir constantly, until the chocolates are melted and smooth. Remove from over the water and set aside to cool slightly.

In a small bowl, stir the cream and instant coffee together until the coffee dissolves. Set aside.

In a large bowl, using an electric mixer on medium speed, beat the butter, powdered (icing) sugar, and salt until smoothly blended and creamy, about 1 minute. On low speed, beat in the melted chocolate, coffee mixture, and vanilla until blended into the frosting. On medium speed, beat the frosting until it is fluffy and lightens slightly in color, about 1 minute. The frosting is best used right after it is made.

ganache and whipped ganache

MAKES 2 CUPS (480 ML) OR 4 CUPS (960 ML)

I am always amazed that simply melting chopped chocolate in hot cream produces something as wonderful as ganache. The ganache can be used warm as a fudge sauce or poured over a cake as a glaze or filling. And that is not all. When lightly whipped, ganache becomes an extraordinary creamy filling.

When whipping ganache, let it cool and thicken to a firm but not hard texture. Refrigerating it will firm it more quickly, but it should chill for only 1 or 2 hours until the edges are firm. Use a whisk to beat the mixture for about 30 seconds until the color lightens from a dark brown to a medium brown. The taste and texture will change from fudgelike to creamlike. Using a whisk prevents the ganache from being whipped too vigorously, which could turn it grainy. Whipped ganache should be spread immediately, as it firms up quickly and becomes difficult to spread smoothly.

✳ Mixing and cooking time 5 minutes

for 2 cups

- 1 CUP (240 ML) HEAVY (DOUBLE) CREAM
- 1 TBSP UNSALTED BUTTER
- 9 OZ (255 G) BITTERSWEET CHOCOLATE, CHOPPED, OR 1½ CUPS (255 G) BITTERSWEET CHOCOLATE CHIPS
- 1 TSP VANILLA EXTRACT (ESSENCE)

for 4 cups

- 2 CUPS (480 ML) HEAVY (DOUBLE) CREAM
- 2 TBSP UNSALTED BUTTER
- 18 OZ (510 G) BITTERSWEET CHOCOLATE, CHOPPED, OR 3 CUPS (510 G) BITTERSWEET CHOCOLATE CHIPS
- 2 TSP VANILLA EXTRACT (ESSENCE)

In a medium saucepan, heat the cream and butter over low heat until the cream is hot and the butter melts. The hot cream mixture should form tiny bubbles and measure about 175°F (80°C) on an instant-read thermometer; do not let the mixture boil as a skin might form on the top. If this happens, use a spoon to lift off the skin and discard it. Remove the pan from the heat, add the chocolate, and let stand in the hot cream mixture for about 30 seconds to soften. Whisk the ganache just until all of the chocolate is melted and the ganache is smooth. Stir in the vanilla.

If the ganache will be poured or spread, let it cool and thicken slightly, about 30 minutes. It can be covered and refrigerated for up to 1 week; if it becomes too firm, it can be warmed over low heat, stirring to soften it evenly.

To make whipped ganache, cover the warm ganache and let stand at room temperature until firm, 3 to 4 hours, depending on the quantity and the temperature of your kitchen. Or, cover and refrigerate the ganache until the edges are firm and the center is slightly thickened, 1 to 2 hours. You can speed up the process to 30 minutes or less by pouring the ganache into a 9-by-13-in (23-by-33-cm) or larger baking dish. Drop a teaspoon of the cold ganache on a plate; set aside to compare the color with that of the beaten ganache. Place the cold ganache in a bowl and whisk until it changes from a dark chocolate color to a medium chocolate color and thickens slightly, about

30 seconds. Compare with the ganache on the plate. The whipped mixture should look lighter in color—similar to a dark, good-quality milk chocolate. Use immediately.

Choices: Other flavorings for ganache include almond extract; ground cinnamon; dissolved instant coffee granules, finely grated orange or lemon zest; fruit purees; and rum, brandy, or other liqueurs. Start with a small quantity, taste the mixture, and keep adding to your taste. Begin with 1 tbsp for the liquor or liqueurs and 1 tsp for instant coffee or grated zest. For almond extract, try ¼ tsp; for cinnamon, ½ tsp, and for fruit purees, 1 tbsp. Quantities can always be increased.

devil's food cake

This is an extremely versatile cake. Two layers can be filled and frosted, or they can be split to form four layers—more filling, more frosting, very good. One large layer can hold a mousse and a glaze; baked as a square, it becomes an informal cake to carry to picnics and barbecues. The cake is dark and moist—and one to bake often.

Use sturdy, good-quality layer pans with sides that are 1¾ to 2 in (4.5 to 5 cm) high. A 9-in (23-cm) square pan should have sides 2 in (5 cm) high.

✳ Mixing time 10 minutes

✳ Baking 350°F (180°C/gas mark 4) for about 35 minutes for 9-in (23-cm) layers, 45 minutes for 10-in (25-cm) layers and a 9-in square cake

for two 9-in layers

- 2   OZ (55 G) UNSWEETENED CHOCOLATE, CHOPPED
- 2   CUPS (225 G) CAKE (SOFT-WHEAT) FLOUR
- ⅔   CUP (60 G) UNSWEETENED DUTCH-PROCESS COCOA POWDER
- 1   TSP BAKING SODA (BICARBONATE OF SODA)
- ½   TSP SALT
- ¾   CUP (170 G) UNSALTED BUTTER, AT ROOM TEMPERATURE
- 1¼   CUPS (250 G) PACKED LIGHT BROWN SUGAR
- ¾   CUP (150 G) GRANULATED SUGAR
- 3   LARGE EGGS
- 1   TSP VANILLA EXTRACT (ESSENCE)
- 1¼   CUPS (300 ML) BUTTERMILK

for one 10-in layer or one 9-in square

- 1½   OZ (40 G) UNSWEETENED CHOCOLATE, CHOPPED
- 1½   CUPS (180 G) CAKE (SOFT-WHEAT) FLOUR
- ½   CUP (45 G) UNSWEETENED DUTCH-PROCESS COCOA POWDER
- ¾   TSP BAKING SODA (BICARBONATE OF SODA)
- ¼   TSP SALT
- ½   CUP (115 G) PLUS 1 TBSP UNSALTED BUTTER, AT ROOM TEMPERATURE
- 1   CUP (200 G) PACKED LIGHT BROWN SUGAR
- ½   CUP (100 G) GRANULATED SUGAR
- 2   LARGE EGGS
- 1   TSP VANILLA EXTRACT (ESSENCE)
- 1   CUP (240 ML) BUTTERMILK

Position a rack in the middle of the oven. Preheat the oven to 350°F (180°C/gas mark 4). Butter the bottom and sides of two 9-in (23-cm) round cake pans, one 10-in (25-cm) cake pan, or one 9-in square pan. Line the bottom(s) with parchment (baking) paper and butter the paper.

Put the chocolate in a heatproof bowl (or the top of a double boiler) and place it over, but not touching, barely simmering water in a saucepan (or the bottom of the double boiler). Stir constantly until the chocolate is melted and smooth. Remove from over the water and set aside to cool slightly.

Sift the flour, cocoa powder, baking soda (bicarbonate of soda), and salt into a medium bowl and set aside. In a large bowl, using an electric mixer on medium speed, beat the butter and brown and granulated sugars until smoothly blended and creamy, about 2 minutes. Stop the mixer and scrape the sides of the bowl as needed. Add the eggs one at a time, mixing until each is blended into the batter. Add the vanilla and beat for 2 minutes. On low speed, mix in the melted chocolate. Add the flour mixture in three additions alternately with the buttermilk in two additions, beginning and ending with the flour mixture and mixing just until the flour is incorporated and the batter looks smooth. Pour the batter into the prepared pan(s), dividing it evenly if more than one pan is used.

Bake just until the top(s) feel firm when lightly touched and a toothpick inserted in the center comes out clean, about 35 minutes for 9-in layers or 45 minutes for a 10-in layer or 9-in square. Cool in the pan(s) on a wire rack for 10 minutes.

Use a small, sharp knife to loosen each cake from the sides of the pan, and invert the cake onto the wire rack. Carefully remove the parchment (baking) paper and place the paper loosely on the cake. Let cool thoroughly, then discard the paper.

white chocolate cake

These light-textured yellow cake layers have the added richness of white chocolate. White chocolate cakes pair exceptionally well with fruit. Some good fruit choices to fill or top a white chocolate cake are peaches, raspberries, strawberries, or blueberries. Use sturdy, good-quality layer pans with sides 1¾ to 2 in (4.5 to 5 cm) high. A 9-in (23-cm) square pan should have sides 2 in (5 cm) high.

❋ Mixing time 10 minutes

❋ Baking 350°F (180°C/gas mark 4) for about 35 minutes for 9-in (23-cm) layers, 40 minutes for 10-in (25-cm) layers and a 9-in square cake

for two 9-in layers		for one 10-in layer or one 9-in square	
1	CUP (240 ML) WHOLE MILK	¾	CUP (180 ML) WHOLE MILK
½	CUP (115 G) UNSALTED BUTTER, CUT INTO 8 PIECES	6	TBSP (85 G) UNSALTED BUTTER, CUT INTO 6 PIECES
8	OZ (225 G) WHITE CHOCOLATE, CHOPPED	6	OZ (170 G) WHITE CHOCOLATE, CHOPPED
2	CUPS (255 G) UNBLEACHED ALL-PURPOSE (PLAIN) FLOUR	1½	CUPS (190 G) UNBLEACHED ALL-PURPOSE (PLAIN) FLOUR
2	TSP BAKING POWDER	1½	TSP BAKING POWDER
½	TSP SALT	¼	TSP SALT
4	LARGE EGGS	3	LARGE EGGS
1¾	CUPS (350 G) SUGAR	1	CUP (200 G) SUGAR
1	TSP VANILLA EXTRACT (ESSENCE)	1	TSP VANILLA EXTRACT (ESSENCE)
2	TSP GRATED ORANGE OR LEMON ZEST (OPTIONAL)	1½	TSP GRATED ORANGE OR LEMON ZEST (OPTIONAL)

Position a rack in the middle of the oven. Preheat the oven to 350°F (180°C/gas mark 4). Butter the bottom and sides of two 9-in (23-cm) round cake pans, one 10-in (25-cm) cake pan, or one 9-in square pan. Line the bottom(s) with parchment (baking) paper and butter the paper.

In a medium saucepan, heat the milk, butter, and white chocolate over low heat. Use a large spoon to stir constantly until the butter and white chocolate are melted and the mixture is smooth. Set aside.

Sift the flour, baking powder, and salt into a medium bowl and set aside. In a large bowl, using an electric mixer on medium speed, beat the eggs and sugar until thickened and lightened to a cream color, about 3 minutes. Stop the mixer and scrape the sides of the bowl as needed. Mix in the vanilla and the orange or lemon zest (if using). On low speed, mix in the flour mixture until it is incorporated. Slowly add the hot milk mixture and continue mixing until the batter is smooth, about 30 seconds. The batter will be thin. Pour the batter into the prepared pan(s), dividing it evenly if more than one pan is used.

Bake just until the top(s) feel firm if lightly touched and a toothpick inserted in the center comes out clean, about 35 minutes for 9-in layers or 40 minutes for a 10-in layer or 9-in square. Cool in the pan(s) on a wire rack for 10 minutes.

Use a small, sharp knife to loosen each cake from the sides of the pan, and invert the cake onto the wire rack. Carefully remove the parchment (baking) paper and place the paper loosely on the cake. Let cool thoroughly, then discard the paper.

chocolate cakes

for a quick chocolate fix

Milk Chocolate Chip–Chocolate Loaf 35 ✳ Pound of Chocolate Cake 37 ✳ Peppermint Patty Cake 39

Hot Chocolate Pudding Cake 40 ✳ Raspberries-on-the-Bottom Cake 41 ✳ S'mores Cake 43

Chocolate Sheet Cake with Chocolate Truffle Glaze 44 ✳ Chocolate-Marzipan Crunch Cake 45

Mint Chocolate Crunch Ice Cream Cake 47 ✳ Milk Chocolate Haystack Ice Cream Loaf 49

Pressed for time—who isn't? Craving chocolate cake—who doesn't? Want cake that is fast to put together—who wouldn't? Then these are the chocolate cakes for you. Each of these ten chocolate cakes can be mixed in 15 minutes or less. Many can be put in the oven when you begin to prepare dinner, then bake while you eat and are ready to be served for dessert. Two ice-cream cakes go together quickly and must be made ahead of time—even a week ahead is fine.

milk chocolate chip– chocolate loaf

Once this loaf cools, it is ready for picnics, snacks, lunch bags, morning coffee, and general chocolate satisfaction. The batter is quite thick—the better to hold the chocolate chips. As a result, chocolate chips float throughout the cake, offering some with every bite.

✳ Mixing time 10 minutes

✳ Baking 325°F (165°C/gas mark 3) for about 1 hour and 10 minutes

---

3	OZ (85 G) UNSWEETENED CHOCOLATE, CHOPPED
1	CUP (130 G) UNBLEACHED ALL-PURPOSE (PLAIN) FLOUR
¼	CUP (25 G) UNSWEETENED DUTCH-PROCESS COCOA POWDER
1	TSP BAKING POWDER
½	TSP BAKING SODA (BICARBONATE OF SODA)
¼	TSP SALT
½	CUP (115 G) UNSALTED BUTTER, AT ROOM TEMPERATURE
1	CUP (200 G) SUGAR
2	LARGE EGGS
¾	CUP (170 G) SOUR CREAM
1	TSP VANILLA EXTRACT (ESSENCE)
½	CUP (120 ML) COFFEE, AT ROOM TEMPERATURE
1½	CUPS (255 G) MILK CHOCOLATE CHIPS
	ICE CREAM FOR SERVING (OPTIONAL)

Position a rack in the middle of the oven. Preheat the oven to 325°F (165°C/gas mark 3). Butter a 9-by-5-by-3-in (23-by-12-by-7.5-cm) loaf pan, or a loaf pan with a capacity of 6 to 8 cups (1.4 to 2 L), and line the bottom with a piece of parchment (baking) paper long enough to extend over the two short sides of the pan. Butter the paper.

Put the unsweetened chocolate in a heatproof bowl (or the top of a double boiler) and place it over, but not touching, barely simmering water in a saucepan (or the bottom of the double boiler). Stir until the chocolate is melted and smooth. Remove from over the water and set aside to cool slightly.

Sift the flour, cocoa powder, baking powder, baking soda (bicarbonate of soda), and salt into a medium bowl and set aside. In a large bowl, using an electric mixer on medium speed, beat the butter and sugar until smoothly blended, about 2 minutes. Stop the mixer and scrape the sides of the bowl as needed. Add the eggs one at a time, beating until each is blended smoothly into the batter and the batter looks creamy, about 2 minutes. Mix in the sour cream and vanilla. On low speed, add half of the flour mixture, mixing just to incorporate it. Mix in the coffee just until blended. Mix in the remaining flour mixture until it is incorporated and the batter looks smooth. Stir in the milk chocolate chips. Scrape the batter into the prepared pan. Gently smooth the top.

Bake until the top feels firm when lightly touched and a toothpick inserted in the center comes out clean, about 1 hour and 10 minutes. If the toothpick penetrates a chocolate chip, test another spot. Let the cake cool completely in the pan on a wire rack, about 1 hour. Use a small, sharp knife to loosen the cake from the sides of the pan, and invert the cake onto the wire rack. Carefully remove and discard the paper. Invert a serving plate on the cake and turn the cake so that it is top up. Cut the cake into slices and serve with scoops of ice cream, if desired.

The cake can be covered and stored at room temperature for up to 2 days.

pound of chocolate cake

This square cake is dark and moist, with a fudge-all-the-way-through texture. What else would you expect from 1 pound (455 g) of chocolate? The cake can be spread with a ganache glaze for even more chocolate richness.

☀ Mixing time 10 minutes

☀ Baking 350°F (180°C/gas mark 4) for about 35 minutes

---

13 OZ (370 G) SEMISWEET (PLAIN) CHOCOLATE, CHOPPED

3 OZ (85 G) UNSWEETENED CHOCOLATE, CHOPPED

¾ CUP (170 G) UNSALTED BUTTER, CUT INTO PIECES

1 TSP INSTANT COFFEE GRANULES DISSOLVED IN
1 TBSP WATER

4 LARGE EGGS

1½ CUPS (300 G) GRANULATED SUGAR

½ TSP SALT

1 TSP VANILLA EXTRACT (ESSENCE)

1 CUP (130 G) UNBLEACHED ALL-PURPOSE (PLAIN) FLOUR

1 CUP (240 ML) GANACHE (PAGE 26), COOLED UNTIL
THICKENED BUT POURABLE (OPTIONAL)

POWDERED (ICING) SUGAR FOR DUSTING (OPTIONAL)

1 QT (960 ML) VANILLA ICE CREAM OR FLAVOR OF YOUR
CHOICE

Position a rack in the middle of the oven. Preheat the oven to 350°F (180°C/gas mark 4). Butter a 9-in (23-cm) square pan with sides 2 in (5 cm) high. Line the bottom with a piece of parchment (baking) paper long enough to extend over opposite sides of the pan. Butter the paper.

Put both chocolates, the butter, and dissolved coffee in a heatproof bowl (or the top of a double boiler) and place it over, but not touching, barely simmering water in a saucepan (or the bottom of the double boiler). Stir until the chocolates and butter are melted and smooth. Remove from over the water and set aside to cool slightly.

In a large bowl, using an electric mixer on medium speed, beat the eggs, sugar, salt, and vanilla until fluffy and lightened in color, about 1 minute. Stop the mixer and scrape the sides of the bowl as needed. On low speed, mix in the melted chocolate mixture until blended. Mix in the flour just until no white streaks remain. Spread the batter evenly in the prepared pan.

Bake until the top of the cake is shiny and firm and a toothpick inserted in the center comes out with moist crumbs clinging to it, about 35 minutes. Cool the cake in the pan on a wire rack for 1 hour.

If using the ganache, pour it over the cake, tilting the pan to spread it evenly. Cool the cake in the pan thoroughly. The cake will become firm. If omitting the glaze, dust the cooled cake with powdered sugar, if desired. Use the overhanging ends of parchment (baking) paper to lift the cake from the pan. Serve the cake at room temperature with scoops of ice cream.

The cake can be covered and stored at room temperature for up to 3 days.

peppermint patty cake

This moist, dense chocolate cake is studded with chocolate-covered peppermint patties, which contribute an intense mint flavor. Crushed peppermint candy adds crunch and a festive touch to the ganache topping.

❉ Mixing time 15 minutes for cake and glaze

❉ Baking 325°F (165°C/gas mark 3) for about 40 minutes

½   CUP (115 G) UNSALTED BUTTER

4   OZ (115 G) UNSWEETENED CHOCOLATE, CHOPPED

1¼   CUPS (160 G) UNBLEACHED ALL-PURPOSE (PLAIN) FLOUR

¾   TSP BAKING POWDER

½   TSP SALT

3   LARGE EGGS

1⅓   CUPS (265 G) SUGAR

1   TSP VANILLA EXTRACT (ESSENCE)

1¼   CUPS (215 G) CHOCOLATE-COVERED PEPPERMINT PATTIES (ABOUT 16), CUT INTO ¾-IN (2-CM) PIECES

2   CUPS (480 ML) GANACHE, COOLED UNTIL THICKENED BUT POURABLE (PAGE 26)

½   CUP (85 G) PEPPERMINT CANDY, CRUSHED INTO SMALL PIECES

Position a rack in the middle of the oven. Preheat the oven to 325°F (165°C/gas mark 3). Butter the bottom and sides of a 9-in (23-cm) round cake pan with sides 1¾ to 2 in (4.5 to 5 cm) high. Line the bottom with parchment (baking) paper and butter the paper.

Put the butter and chocolate in a heatproof bowl (or the top of a double boiler) and place it over, but not touching, barely simmering water in a saucepan (or the bottom of the double boiler). Stir until the chocolate and butter are melted and smooth. Remove from over the water and set aside to cool slightly.

In a medium bowl, stir the flour, baking powder, and salt together. Set aside. In a large bowl, using an electric mixer on medium speed, beat the eggs, sugar, and vanilla until light and fluffy, about 1 minute. Stop the mixer and scrape the sides of the bowl as needed. On low speed, mix in the melted chocolate mixture until blended. Mix in the flour mixture just until it is incorporated. Stir in the peppermint patties. Pour the batter into the prepared pan, smoothing the top with a spatula.

Bake until a toothpick inserted in the center comes out with moist crumbs clinging to it, about 40 minutes. Cool the cake in the pan on a wire rack for 15 minutes. Use a small, sharp knife to loosen the cake from the sides of the pan, and invert the cake onto a wire rack. Carefully remove the paper and loosely place on the cake. Let cool thoroughly, then discard the paper.

Invert the cake onto a serving plate so that it is top up. Use a small spatula to spread the ganache over the top and sides of the cake. Let the glaze set and firm up for about 15 minutes. Sprinkle the crushed candy over the top of the cake.

The cake can be covered and stored at room temperature for up to 2 days, but add the candy topping at serving time.

hot chocolate pudding cake

Step aside all lava cakes, hot chocolate cakes, and molten chocolate cakes. This magical cake will astonish with its ease, mystify with its ability to be baked into a sauce plus cake, and satisfy without question.

☼ Mixing time 5 minutes

☼ Baking 350°F (180°C/gas mark 4) for about 40 minutes

---

1   CUP (130 G) UNBLEACHED ALL-PURPOSE (PLAIN) FLOUR

¾   CUP (150 G) GRANULATED SUGAR

½   CUP (50 G) UNSWEETENED DUTCH-PROCESS COCOA POWDER

1½ TSP BAKING POWDER

¼   TSP SALT

½   CUP (120 ML) WHOLE MILK

3   TBSP UNSALTED BUTTER, MELTED

1   CUP (170 G) SEMISWEET (PLAIN) CHOCOLATE CHIPS

1   TSP VANILLA EXTRACT (ESSENCE)

1   CUP (200 G) PACKED LIGHT BROWN SUGAR

1¾ CUPS (420 ML) HOT COFFEE

    VANILLA ICE CREAM OR WHIPPED CREAM FOR SERVING (OPTIONAL)

Position a rack in the middle of the oven. Preheat the oven to 350°F (180°C/gas mark 4). Have ready an 8-in (20-cm) square pan.

Sift the flour, sugar, ¼ cup (25 g) of the cocoa powder, the baking powder, and salt into a medium bowl. Stir in the milk, melted butter, chocolate chips, and vanilla until smoothly blended. Spread the batter (it will be thick) in the pan. In a small bowl, stir the brown sugar and the remaining ¼ cup cocoa powder together, pressing any lumps out of the brown sugar. Sprinkle the brown sugar mixture evenly over the batter in the pan. Pour the hot coffee evenly over the top.

Bake until the top feels firm and the edges just begin to bubble from the sauce that has formed underneath, about 40 minutes. As the cake bakes, it separates into dark chocolate sauce on the bottom and chocolate cake on top. Cool the cake in the pan on a wire rack for about 30 minutes. Spoon out portions of cake and sauce. Serve with vanilla ice cream, if desired.

The cake can be made up to 1 day ahead and heated in a 275°F (135°C/gas mark 1) oven until warm.

Choices: Milk chocolate or bittersweet chocolate chips can be substituted for the semisweet (plain) chocolate chips.

raspberries-on-the-bottom cake

At first glance, this cake looks quite plain. Then, cutting a slice reveals the raspberries and their sauce saturating the bottom. Be sure to use a glass or ceramic baking dish that will not react with the acidic raspberries.

※ Mixing time 10 minutes

※ Baking 350°F (180°C/gas mark 4) for about 35 minutes

2	CUPS (225 G) FRESH RASPBERRIES, PLUS RASPBERRIES FOR SERVING
¾	CUP (150 G) SUGAR, PLUS 2 TSP
1¼	CUPS (160 G) UNBLEACHED ALL-PURPOSE (PLAIN) FLOUR
¼	CUP (25 G) UNSWEETENED DUTCH-PROCESS COCOA POWDER
1	TSP BAKING POWDER
¼	TSP SALT
½	CUP (115 G) UNSALTED BUTTER, SOFTENED
1	LARGE EGG
1	TSP VANILLA EXTRACT (ESSENCE)
¼	TSP ALMOND EXTRACT (ESSENCE)
½	CUP (120 ML) WHOLE MILK

Position a rack in the middle of the oven. Preheat the oven to 350°F (180°C/gas mark 4). Have ready a 9-in (23-cm) round glass or ceramic baking dish with sides 2 in (5 cm) high. A deep glass pie dish will work well.

Spoon the 2 cups (225 g) raspberries evenly into the baking dish. Sprinkle with the 2 tsp sugar. Set aside.

Sift the flour, cocoa powder, baking powder, and salt into a medium bowl and set aside. In a large bowl, using an electric mixer on medium speed, beat the butter and the ¾ cup (150 g) sugar until smoothly blended, about 1 minute. Stop the mixer and scrape the sides of the bowl as needed. Add the egg, vanilla, and almond extract (essence) and mix until smoothly blended, about 1 minute. On low speed, add half of the flour mixture, mixing just to incorporate it. Mix in the milk just until blended. Mix in the remaining flour mixture until it is incorporated and the batter looks smooth. Drop spoonfuls of batter over the raspberries and use a spatula to spread it carefully and evenly.

Bake until the top feels firm when lightly touched and a toothpick inserted in the center comes out clean, about 35 minutes. The raspberries will just begin to bubble at the edges. Cool the cake in the dish on a wire rack for at least 30 minutes. Cut into wedges, spooning any raspberries and their juice over the cake. Serve with fresh raspberries.

The cake can be covered and left at room temperature for 1 day.

s'mores cake

Some serious decision making is involved here. Do you eat this cake warm or let it cool? The warm cake is a soft, almost falling-apart graham-cracker cake, filled with melted milk chocolate and topped with melted marshmallows. When cool, the cake is slightly sticky, the milk chocolate is soft, and the marshmallows flatten and form a sticky, glazed topping. Whatever state you choose, you can't go wrong. Boxes of graham cracker crumbs can be found in the baking section of supermarkets.

❋ Mixing time 10 minutes

❋ Baking 325°F (165°C/gas mark 3) for about 35 minutes

---

2   CUPS (200 G) GRAHAM CRACKER CRUMBS

¼   CUP (30 G) UNBLEACHED ALL-PURPOSE (PLAIN) FLOUR

1½ TSP BAKING POWDER

¼   TSP SALT

½   CUP (115 G) UNSALTED BUTTER, AT ROOM TEMPERATURE

¾   CUP (150 G) SUGAR

3   LARGE EGGS

2   TSP VANILLA EXTRACT (ESSENCE)

¾   CUP (180 ML) WHOLE MILK

1   LB (455 G) MILK CHOCOLATE CANDY BARS, BROKEN INTO 1-IN (2.5-CM) PIECES

15 MARSHMALLOWS

Position a rack in the middle of the oven. Preheat the oven to 325°F (165°C/gas mark 3). Line the bottom and sides of a 13-by-9-in (33-by-23-cm) baking pan with a piece of aluminum foil long enough to extend over all sides of the pan. Butter the foil. The cake is sticky, and lining the entire pan makes the cake easier to remove.

Put the graham cracker crumbs in a medium bowl. Sift the flour, baking powder, and salt over the crumbs and stir to combine. Set aside.

In a large bowl, using an electric mixer on medium speed, beat the butter and sugar until the mixture looks creamy and lightens in color, about 2 minutes. Stop the mixer and scrape the sides of the bowl as needed. Add the eggs one a time, beating well after each addition. Mix in the vanilla. On low speed, add half of the crumb mixture, mixing just to incorporate it. Mix in the milk just until blended. Mix in the remaining crumb mixture just until it is incorporated. Stir in the milk chocolate pieces. Scrape the batter into the prepared pan.

Bake for 20 minutes. Remove the pan from the oven. Arrange the marshmallows on top of the cake, placing them in three rows across the length of the cake, with each row containing five marshmallows; allow about 1½ in (4 cm) between the marshmallows and leave a 1-in (2.5-cm) border around the edge of the cake uncovered. Continue baking until the marshmallows are light golden and puffed and a toothpick inserted into the center of the cake comes out with just a few crumbs clinging to it, about 15 minutes.

Immediately use a small, sharp knife to loosen the cake from the sides of the pan, then let the cake cool in the pan on a wire rack for 30 minutes. The cake can be served warm, or it can be cooled completely, at least 4 hours or up to overnight, and served at room temperature. As the cake cools, the marshmallows deflate, but retain their round shape.

To serve the cake, lift the foil and cake from the pan, cut the cake into squares, and use a spatula to slide the squares off the foil.

The cake can be covered carefully and stored at room temperature for up to 2 days.

chocolate sheet cake with chocolate truffle glaze

"Easiest cake to mix" is what I wrote on my testing notes the first time I made this recipe. Mixing is as simple as putting all of the ingredients into a bowl, stirring them until they are smooth, and pouring the batter into a large pan and baking. This is a great cake for serving a crowd, and it can easily be transported right in its pan. That makes it a good choice for picnics, family reunions, and potlucks.

* Mixing time 15 minutes for cake and frosting
* Baking 325°F (165°C/gas mark 3) for about 25 minutes

2	OZ (55 G) UNSWEETENED CHOCOLATE, CHOPPED
¾	CUP (170 G) UNSALTED BUTTER, CUT INTO PIECES
2	CUPS (225 G) CAKE (SOFT-WHEAT) FLOUR
⅓	CUP (30 G) UNSWEETENED DUTCH-PROCESS COCOA POWDER
1½	CUPS (300 G) SUGAR
½	TSP BAKING POWDER
¾	TSP BAKING SODA (BICARBONATE OF SODA)
⅛	TSP SALT
3	LARGE EGGS
1	TSP VANILLA EXTRACT (ESSENCE)
1	CUP (240 ML) WATER
2	CUPS (480 ML) GANACHE (PAGE 26), COOLED AND AT SPREADING CONSISTENCY
1	QT (960 ML) ICE CREAM FOR SERVING (OPTIONAL)

Position a rack in the middle of the oven. Preheat the oven to 325°F (165°C/gas mark 3). Butter a 13-by-9-by-2-in (33-by-23-by-5-cm) pan.

Put the chocolate and butter in a heatproof bowl (or the top of a double boiler) and place it over, but not touching, barely simmering water in a saucepan (or the bottom of the double boiler). Stir until the butter and chocolate are melted and smooth.

Pour the melted chocolate mixture into a large bowl. Sift the flour, cocoa powder, sugar, baking powder, baking soda (bicarbonate of soda), and salt into the bowl. Add the eggs, vanilla, and water and mix on low speed until the batter is smooth and shiny and all of the flour is incorporated, about 1 minute. Spread the batter evenly in the prepared pan.

Bake the cake until the top feels firm when lightly touched and a toothpick inserted in the center comes out clean, about 25 minutes. Cool the cake in the pan on a wire rack.

Pour the ganache over the cooled cake and tilt the pan gently to spread it evenly. Cut the cake into squares and serve with ice cream, if desired.

The cake can be covered and stored at room temperature for up to 2 days.

chocolate-marzipan crunch cake

This cake has a crisp bottom, a soft almond filling that resembles marzipan candy, and crisp crumbs on top. The bottom of the cake and the crumb topping are made from the same batter. When freshly baked, this cake is soft, but after sitting overnight, it becomes crisp while the marzipan filling remains soft. Be sure to buy almond paste rather than marzipan, which contains more sugar than almond paste. Almond paste in cans or sealed plastic tubes is available in the baking section of most supermarkets.

✳ Mixing time 10 minutes

✳ Baking 375°F (190°C/gas mark 5) for about 30 minutes

filling

½ CUP (100 G) SUGAR

ABOUT 1 CUP (225 G) ALMOND PASTE, AT ROOM TEMPERATURE, BROKEN INTO PIECES

¼ CUP (55 G) UNSALTED BUTTER, AT ROOM TEMPERATURE

1 LARGE EGG WHITE

1 TBSP FRESH LEMON JUICE

cake

2¾ CUPS (355 G) UNBLEACHED ALL-PURPOSE (PLAIN) FLOUR

½ CUP (45 G) UNSWEETENED DUTCH-PROCESS COCOA POWDER

1 TSP BAKING POWDER

½ TSP SALT

½ CUP (115 G) PLUS 6 TBSP (85 G) UNSALTED BUTTER, SOFTENED FOR 30 MINUTES

1 CUP (200 G) SUGAR

1 LARGE EGG

1 TSP GRATED LEMON ZEST

1 TSP VANILLA EXTRACT (ESSENCE)

Position a rack in the middle of the oven. Preheat the oven to 375°F (190°C/gas mark 5). Butter a 9-in (23-cm) springform pan with sides at least 2¾ in (7 cm) high.

To make the filling: In a food processor, process the sugar for about 15 seconds to grind it more finely. Add the almond paste, butter, egg white, and lemon juice and process until blended smoothly, about 20 seconds. Scrape into a small bowl and set aside.

To make the cake: Sift the flour, cocoa powder, baking powder, and salt into a medium bowl and set aside. In a large bowl, using an electric mixer on low speed, beat the butter and sugar until blended smoothly, about 1 minute. Mix in the egg, lemon zest, and vanilla. Add the flour mixture, mixing just until crumbs form and all of the flour is incorporated. Press half of the crumb mixture onto the bottom and ½ in (12 mm) up the sides of the prepared pan. Use a small spatula to spread the almond filling over the crumb mixture. Sprinkle the remaining crumb mixture evenly over the filling.

Bake until the crumb topping feels firm when touched lightly, about 30 minutes. At first, the topping will look shiny and melted, then, as the cake cools, it will look dry. Let the cake cool in the pan on a wire rack for about 1 hour.

Use a small, sharp knife to loosen the sides of the cake from the pan, then remove the sides. Use the knife to loosen the cake from the bottom of the pan. With a wide metal spatula, slide the cake onto a platter.

The cake can be covered and stored at room temperature for up to 2 days.

mint chocolate crunch
ice cream cake

This is the cake to serve after a big holiday dinner or any time you want an especially refreshing dessert. It is like a giant after-dinner ice cream mint. The cake has two crunchy layers of crushed store-bought chocolate mint sandwich cookies combined with chocolate: one between layers of ice cream and the other topping the cake. The easiest way to crush the sandwich cookies is to put them in a plastic bag and use a rolling pin to make coarse crumbs. It is best to do this in two batches. This method is preferred over using a food processor, which could turn the filled cookies into a paste.

※ Mixing time 10 minutes

※ Baking 325°F (165°C/gas mark 3) for 6 minutes

chocolate crumb crust

ONE 9-OZ (255-G) PACKAGE CHOCOLATE WAFERS, PROCESSED TO CRUMBS IN A FOOD PROCESSOR (ABOUT 2 CUPS TOTAL)

6 **TBSP (85 G) UNSALTED BUTTER, MELTED**

mint chocolate crunch

2 **CUPS (250 G) COARSELY CRUSHED CHOCOLATE MINT SANDWICH COOKIES (SUCH AS 20 PEPPERIDGE FARM CHOCOLATE MINT MILANO COOKIES)**

4 **OZ (115 G) SEMISWEET (PLAIN) CHOCOLATE, CHOPPED**

1 **TBSP CORN OR CANOLA OIL**

2 **QT (2 L) MINT CHOCOLATE CHIP OR PEPPERMINT ICE CREAM, SOFTENED JUST UNTIL SPREADABLE**

Position a rack in the middle of the oven. Preheat the oven to 325°F (165°C/gas mark 3). Butter a 9-in (23-cm) springform pan with sides at least 2¾ in (7 cm) high.

To make the crust: In a large bowl, stir the wafer crumbs and melted butter together to moisten the crumbs evenly. Scrape the crumb mixture into the prepared pan. Using the back of your fingers or the back of a spoon, press the crumb mixture evenly over the bottom and 1 in (2.5 cm) up the sides

of the pan. Be careful not to make the crust too thick on the bottom where it meets the sides. Bake for 6 minutes. Let cool thoroughly before adding the ice cream.

To make the mint chocolate crunch: Line a baking sheet (tray) with parchment (baking) paper. Put the cookie crumbs in a large bowl and set aside. Put the chocolate and the oil in a heatproof bowl (or the top of a double boiler) and place it over, but not touching, barely simmering water in a saucepan (or the bottom of the double boiler). Stir until the chocolate is melted and smooth.

Pour the melted chocolate over the cookie crumbs and stir until the crumbs are coated evenly. The mixture will look shiny and form pieces that vary from about ¼ in (6 mm) to ½ in (12 mm). Spread the crumb mixture on the prepared baking sheet. As it cools, it will turn from shiny to dull and become crisp. You will have about 3 cups (365 g) mint chocolate crunch.

Use an ice cream spade to spread half of the ice cream in the cooled crust. Smooth the top. Sprinkle evenly with half of the mint chocolate crunch. Spread the remaining ice cream over the crunch. Sprinkle evenly with the remaining crunch. Wrap the cake, in its pan, tightly in plastic wrap (cling film) and then in heavy aluminum foil. Freeze overnight or for up to 1 week.

To serve the cake, unwrap it, and use a thin, sharp knife to loosen the cake from the sides of the pan. Remove the sides, and use a large, sharp knife to cut the cake into slices.

Choices: Substitute chocolate or vanilla ice cream for the mint ice cream.

milk chocolate haystack ice cream loaf

Ice cream makes great layer cakes. This one has milk chocolate and toasted coconut "haystacks" between layers of chocolate and coffee ice cream.

❋ Mixing time 15 minutes

❋ Baking 325°F (165°C/gas mark 3) for about 20 minutes

2½ CUPS (210 G) SWEETENED SHREDDED COCONUT

9 OZ (255 G) MILK CHOCOLATE, CHOPPED

1 TBSP CORN OR CANOLA OIL

1 QT (960 ML) CHOCOLATE ICE CREAM, SOFTENED JUST UNTIL SPREADABLE

1 PT (480 ML) COFFEE ICE CREAM, SOFTENED JUST UNTIL SPREADABLE

Preheat the oven to 325°F (165°C/gas mark 3). Spread the coconut on a baking sheet (tray). Bake, stirring once, until the coconut turns golden, about 20 minutes. Remove the coconut from the oven and set aside.

Put the chocolate and oil in a heatproof bowl (or the top of a double boiler) and place it over, but not touching, barely simmering water in a saucepan (or the bottom of the double boiler). Stir constantly until the chocolate is melted and blended smoothly with the oil. Remove from over the water. Stir 1½ cups (125 g) of the toasted coconut into the chocolate mixture. Put the remaining 1 cup (85 g) toasted coconut in a bowl, cover tightly, and set aside at room temperature for use after the cake is unmolded. Put ¾ cup (180 ml) of the coconut-chocolate haystack mixture in another bowl, cover tightly, and set aside at room temperature for use after the cake is unmolded.

Line the bottom of a 9-by-5-by-3-in (23-by-12-by-7.5-cm) loaf pan, or a loaf pan with a capacity of 6 to 8 cups (1.4 to 2 L), with a piece of parchment (baking) paper long enough to extend over the two short sides of the pan.

Use an ice cream spade to spread half of the chocolate ice cream in an even layer in the bottom of the prepared pan, spreading it carefully to the edges. Using half of the haystack mixture, drop spoonfuls over the ice cream. Spread evenly with the coffee ice cream, then top with spoonfuls of the remaining haystack mixture. Spread with the remaining chocolate ice cream. Cover tightly with plastic wrap (cling film) and freeze for at least 5 hours or up to overnight.

Chill a serving plate for about 15 minutes before unmolding the cake. Remove the cake from the freezer and unwrap it. Use a thin, sharp knife to loosen the ice cream from the sides of the pan. Dip a kitchen towel in hot water and wring out. Press the hot towel onto the sides of the pan for about 25 seconds. Place the chilled serving plate on top of the loaf and invert the loaf onto the plate, pulling on the ends of the paper. Discard the paper. Drop teaspoons of the reserved haystack mixture onto the top of the ice cream, pressing it into the loaf. If the chocolate has hardened, warm the haystack mixture over low heat just to soften it. Sprinkle the reserved toasted coconut over the top of the loaf, pressing some of the coconut onto the sides of the cake.

To serve the cake, use a large, sharp knife to cut the loaf into slices a scant 1 in (2.5 cm) thick.

The cake can be stored wrapped tightly with plastic wrap (cling film) and frozen for up to 1 week.

Choices: Other ice cream combinations are chocolate and vanilla; chocolate and chocolate chip; and chocolate and coconut.

big
one-layer
chocolate
cakes

These cakes are big in two ways. Some are big in size, at least 3 in (7.5 cm) high, and are baked in a tube, Bundt, springform, or loaf pan. Others, such as the Raspberry and White Chocolate Truffle Cake, are smaller one-layer cakes that pack a wallop of flavor.

Bundt and tube pans have a center tube that helps large cakes bake evenly. A standard loaf pan is 9 by 5 in (23 by 12 cm), but these pans come in many sizes, so I include capacity whenever I use loaf pans.

To ensure that cakes release cleanly, I line the smooth bottoms of tube and loaf pans with parchment (baking) paper. The patterned bottom of a Bundt pan cannot be lined, and that is why it is important to use a heavyweight Bundt pan. It is frustrating to turn a Bundt cake out of the pan and have part of the cake stick—believe me, I know. I rub oil carefully inside the Bundt pan with a pastry brush or paper towel and then sprinkle the pan with flour and tap out any extra. Because Bundt pans have patterns, you must be careful that oil and flour do not puddle in any of the indentations on the bottom. If after all of your precautions a Bundt cake does stick to the pan, a warm fragment of cake left in the pan can often be pressed back into the unmolded cake. Or, if the cake has a glaze, you can use a bit of it to "glue" the piece in place. Bundt cakes are served bottom up, allowing the pattern to show.

Some tube cakes, such as the Chinese Five-Spice Chocolate Chiffon Cake, are served bottom up, which provides a smooth top and a sharp edge for applying a glaze.

A long, wide spatula works well for moving these large cakes from a wire rack to a platter. Slide the spatula under the bottom of the cake, place the platter level with the cake, and slide the cake onto the platter. I find it safer to move a cake after it has cooled thoroughly and before adding a glaze.

raspberry and white chocolate truffle cake

This is my ugly duckling cake. When baked, it looks okay, though not terribly gorgeous, but with the first bite, it becomes a beautiful swan. The texture is soft, and the abundance of white chocolate makes for an intense flavor. Swirls of pureed raspberries provide a taste and color contrast. It is no fairy tale.

✳ Mixing time 20 minutes for cake and raspberry puree

✳ Baking 375°F (190°C/gas mark 5) for about 35 minutes

---

1   LB (455 G) WHITE CHOCOLATE, CHOPPED

½   CUP (115 G) UNSALTED BUTTER, CUT INTO 8 PIECES

1½ CUPS (170 G) FRESH OR DEFROSTED, FROZEN
     UNSWEETENED RASPBERRIES, PLUS RASPBERRIES
     FOR SERVING

2   TBSP SUGAR, PLUS 1 TSP

4   LARGE EGGS, SEPARATED

2   TBSP UNBLEACHED ALL-PURPOSE (PLAIN) FLOUR

1   TSP VANILLA EXTRACT (ESSENCE)

¼   TSP ALMOND EXTRACT (ESSENCE)

¼   TSP CREAM OF TARTAR

Position a rack in the middle of the oven. Preheat the oven to 375°F (190°C/gas mark 5). Remove the bottom of an 8-in (20-cm) springform pan with sides at least 2¾ in (7 cm) high, and wrap it with heavy aluminum foil. Replace the bottom. Butter the bottom and sides of the pan. Wrap the outside of the pan with a large piece of heavy foil to catch any drips that escape between the bottom and sides during baking.

Put the white chocolate and butter in a heatproof bowl (or the top of a double boiler) and place it over, but not touching, barely simmering water in a saucepan (or the bottom of the double boiler). Stir until the chocolate and butter melt and are blended smoothly. Scrape the mixture into a large bowl and set aside to cool slightly.

Process the 1½ cups (170 g) raspberries to a puree in a food processor. Strain the puree into a small bowl, pressing with the back of a spoon to help push it through the strainer. Discard any seeds or pulp in the strainer. Measure ¼ cup (60 ml) puree for the filling and stir in the 1 tsp sugar. Set aside. If any puree remains, save it for another use.

Whisk the egg yolks into the chocolate mixture to blend them. Whisk in the flour, vanilla, and almond extract (essence).

In a clean large bowl, using an electric mixer on low speed, beat the egg whites and cream of tartar until the whites are foamy and the cream of tartar dissolves. On medium speed, beat the egg whites until they look shiny and smooth and the movement of the beaters forms lines in the mixture. When you stop the mixer and lift the beaters, the beaten whites should cling to them. Beat in the 2 tbsp sugar, then beat for 1 minute.

Use a rubber spatula to fold one-third of the beaten whites into the white chocolate mixture to lighten it. Then fold in the remaining whites. Pour the batter into the prepared pan. Spoon the raspberry puree in swirling lines over the batter. Use a small knife to swirl it through the batter.

Bake until the cake is browned on top, the edges are firm, and the center is softly set, about 35 minutes. If you give the cake a gentle jiggle, the center will wobble slightly. Use a small, sharp knife to loosen the sides of the cake from the pan. Remove the foil from the outside of the pan and discard it. Cool the cake in the pan on a wire rack for 1 hour. As it cools, the cake will sink slightly in the center, forming raised edges. Refrigerate the cake until it is firm, about 2 hours.

Remove the sides of the springform pan. Invert the chilled cake onto a wire rack. Remove the bottom of the pan. Invert a serving platter on the cake and turn the cake so that it is top up. Slice the cake and serve cold with fresh raspberries. The center of the cake remains soft even when cold.

The cake can be covered and refrigerated for up to 3 days.

double-glazed espresso and chocolate cake

MAKES 12 SERVINGS

A sweet coffee syrup drenches this chocolate-espresso cake, which is then covered in a luscious chocolate glaze. Bundt cake pans make beautifully patterned cakes, but careful pan preparation is key to having the cake release easily from the pan. Choose a heavy Bundt pan, preferably with a nonstick finish. Then grease the pan carefully with oil, taking care that all of the patterned crevices and the center tube are thoroughly oiled. Dust the pan with flour, which will cling to the greased pan.

❊ Mixing time 20 minutes for cake and glazes

❊ Baking 325°F (165°C/gas mark 3) for about 1 hour

cake

3 OZ (85 G) UNSWEETENED CHOCOLATE, CHOPPED

2¾ CUPS (355 G) UNBLEACHED ALL-PURPOSE (PLAIN) FLOUR

1 TSP BAKING POWDER

1 TSP BAKING SODA (BICARBONATE OF SODA)

½ TSP SALT

¾ CUP (170 G) UNSALTED BUTTER, AT ROOM TEMPERATURE

2 CUPS (400 G) SUGAR

4 LARGE EGGS

2 TSP VANILLA EXTRACT (ESSENCE)

2 TBSP INSTANT ESPRESSO GRANULES DISSOLVED IN 1¼ CUPS (420 ML) WATER

coffee syrup

1 TBSP INSTANT ESPRESSO GRANULES

¼ CUP (50 G) SUGAR

½ CUP (120 ML) WATER

chocolate glaze

⅓ CUP (75 ML) HEAVY (DOUBLE) CREAM

¼ CUP (55 G) UNSALTED BUTTER, CUT INTO PIECES

2 TSP LIGHT CORN (GOLDEN) SYRUP

9 OZ (255 G) SEMISWEET (PLAIN) CHOCOLATE, CHOPPED

1 TSP VANILLA EXTRACT (ESSENCE)

Position a rack in the middle of the oven. Preheat the oven to 325°F (165°C/gas mark 3). Oil a Bundt pan with a capacity of 3 qt (2.8 L), then sprinkle flour lightly inside the pan and tilt the pan to coat it evenly. Tap out and discard any loose flour.

To make the cake: Put the chocolate in a heatproof bowl (or the top of a double boiler) and place it over, but not touching, barely simmering water in a saucepan (or the bottom of the double boiler). Stir until the chocolate is melted and smooth. Remove from over the water and set aside to cool slightly.

Sift the flour, baking powder, baking soda (bicarbonate of soda), and salt into a medium bowl and set aside. In a large bowl, using an electric mixer on medium speed, beat the butter and sugar until fluffy and smooth, about 3 minutes. Stop the mixer and scrape the sides of the bowl as needed. Add the eggs two at a time, mixing until each addition is blended into the batter, and adding the vanilla with the last addition. Beat for 1 minute more. On low speed, mix in the chocolate. Add the flour mixture in three additions and the espresso in two additions, beginning and ending with the flour mixture and mixing just until the flour is incorporated and the batter looks smooth. Pour the batter into the prepared pan and gently smooth the top.

Bake until a toothpick inserted in the center comes out clean or with just a few crumbs clinging to it, about 1 hour. Cool the cake in the pan on a wire rack for 10 minutes. Use a small, sharp knife to loosen the cake from the edges and center tube of the pan. Let the cake cool for 20 minutes, then invert it onto the wire rack, tapping the bottom several times if it does not release immediately.

To make the coffee syrup: In a small saucepan, heat the espresso, sugar, and water over medium heat, stirring constantly until the sugar dissolves. Set the syrup aside.

As soon as the cake is released from the pan, use a toothpick to poke holes in the top and sides of the cake. Use a pastry brush to brush all of the syrup evenly over the cake. Let the cake cool completely on the wire rack.

To make the chocolate glaze: Combine the cream, butter, and corn (golden) syrup in a medium saucepan. Cook over medium heat until the butter melts and the mixture is hot. Remove from the heat, add the chocolate, and let them sit in the hot cream mixture for 1 minute. Stir until the chocolate melts and the glaze is smooth. Stir in the vanilla. Set aside at room temperature for about 20 minutes to cool and thicken slightly so the glaze will cling to the cake.

Use a large spatula to transfer the cooled cake to a serving plate. Tuck wax (greaseproof) paper strips 1 in (2.5 cm) or so under the cake all the way around to keep the plate clean. Gently pour about half of the glaze over the top of the cake. Use a thin metal spatula to spread the glaze inside the hole in the center and over the top and sides of the cake. Pour any remaining glaze on top of the cake and spread it evenly. Remove the paper strips and discard them.

Once the glaze is firm, the cake can be covered and stored at room temperature for up to 3 days.

chocolate and peanut butter mousse cake

MAKES 12 TO 14 SERVINGS

We are talking serious cake here. The baked cake layer, a combination of devil's food and pieces of peanut butter cups, is spooned out of the center, and the cavity is filled with peanut butter mousse and pieces of the scooped-out cake. Ganache and more peanut butter cup pieces cover the cake. As I told you, it is a serious cake.

✳ Mixing time 30 minutes for cake, mousse, and ganache
✳ Baking 350°F (180°C/gas mark 4) for about 40 minutes

---

8   OZ (230 G) PEANUT BUTTER CUPS; 4 OZ (115 G) CUT INTO ½-IN (12-MM) PIECES, 4 OZ (115 G) COARSELY CHOPPED

FRESHLY MIXED BATTER FOR ONE 10-IN (25-CM) DEVIL'S FOOD CAKE LAYER (PAGE 28)

peanut butter mousse

6   OZ (170 G) CREAM CHEESE, AT ROOM TEMPERATURE

¾   CUP (210 G) CREAMY PEANUT BUTTER, AT ROOM TEMPERATURE

¾   CUP (75 G) POWDERED (ICING) SUGAR

1   CUP (240 ML) COLD HEAVY (DOUBLE) CREAM

1   TSP VANILLA EXTRACT (ESSENCE)

2   CUPS (480 ML) GANACHE (PAGE 26), COOLED UNTIL THICKENED BUT POURABLE

Preheat the oven to 350°F (180°C/gas mark 4). Butter the bottom and sides of a 10-in (25-cm) round cake pan. Line the bottom with parchment (baking) paper and butter the paper.

Use a rubber spatula to stir the 4 oz (115 g) cup of peanut butter pieces into the cake batter. Pour the batter into the prepared pan. Bake until the top feels firm when lightly touched and a toothpick inserted in the center comes out clean, about 40 minutes. Cool the cake in the pan on a wire rack for 10 minutes.

Use a small, sharp knife to loosen the cake from the sides of the pan, and invert the cake onto the wire rack. Carefully remove the paper, then place it loosely on the cake. Let the cake cool thoroughly, then discard the paper.

To make the peanut butter mousse: In a large bowl, using an electric mixer on medium speed, beat the cream cheese and peanut butter until smoothly blended. On low speed, mix in the powdered (icing) sugar until it is incorporated. The texture will not look completely smooth. Set aside.

In a clean large bowl, using clean beaters, beat the cream and vanilla on medium-high speed until firm peaks form. Whisk about one-third of the whipped cream into the peanut butter mixture. Use a rubber spatula to gently but thoroughly fold in the remaining whipped cream. The mousse will be smooth.

Invert the cake onto a serving plate so that it is top up. Leaving a 1-in (2.5-cm) plain edge around the top of the cake, use a small, sharp knife to cut out the center in one piece to create a cavity about 1 in (2.5 cm) deep. Break the removed cake into pieces about 1 in (2.5 cm). Use a metal spatula to spread about one-third of the mousse in the hollowed-out center of the cake. Put the cake pieces over the mousse, mounding them toward the center. Spread the remaining mousse over the cake pieces. It will cover the cake. Refrigerate the cake until the mousse is firm, about 30 minutes.

Use a spatula to spread the ganache over the top and sides of the cake. Scatter the 4 oz (115 g) chopped peanut butter cups over the ganache. Use a large, sharp knife to cut the cake, carefully wiping it clean after cutting each slice. Serve cold.

The cake can be covered and refrigerated for up to 2 days.

chinese five-spice chocolate chiffon cake

Cinnamon, aniseed, cloves, ginger, and fennel seed may sound like an odd combination. Not so. These spices are ground together to make Chinese five-spice powder. The blend adds a mysterious, subtle, and appealing flavor to chocolate and to this moist, light chiffon cake. The seasoning is also sprinkled lightly over the glaze. Look for jars of the powder in the spice section of supermarkets.

Chiffon cakes bake in a large ungreased tube pan. This allows the cake to climb up the sides of the pan and remain there while it cools. I once greased a pan by mistake. The cake rose extremely high, then slid down the pan and collapsed as soon as it came out of the oven. Chiffon cakes cool in the pan upside down so they do not collapse under their own weight. This tall cake is delicate when warm, but quite sturdy once it cools.

✳ Mixing time 15 minutes for cake and glaze

✳ Baking 325°F (165°C/gas mark 3) for about 1 hour and 10 minutes

cake

1¾ CUPS (205 G) CAKE (SOFT-WHEAT) FLOUR

½ CUP (45 G) UNSWEETENED DUTCH-PROCESS COCOA POWDER

1½ CUPS (300 G) SUGAR

2½ TSP CHINESE FIVE-SPICE POWDER

½ TSP GROUND CINNAMON

2 TSP BAKING POWDER

½ TSP SALT

½ CUP (120 ML) CANOLA OR CORN OIL

7 LARGE EGGS, SEPARATED

¾ CUP (180 ML) WATER

1½ TSP VANILLA EXTRACT (ESSENCE)

1 TSP CREAM OF TARTAR

6 OZ (170 G) MILK CHOCOLATE, FINELY CHOPPED

glaze

⅓ CUP (75 ML) HEAVY (DOUBLE) CREAM

1 TSP CORN (GOLDEN) SYRUP

6 OZ (170 G) MILK CHOCOLATE, CHOPPED

1 TSP VANILLA EXTRACT (ESSENCE)

¾ TSP CHINESE FIVE-SPICE POWDER FOR DUSTING

12 DARK CHOCOLATE STRIPS (SEE PAGE 13), EACH ABOUT 2 BY ⅜ IN (5 BY 1 CM)

Preheat the oven to 325°F (165°C/gas mark 3). Have ready a 9½- or 10-in (24- or 25-cm) fixed-bottom tube pan with sides at least 3¾ in (9.5 cm) high. Do not use a nonstick pan. Line the bottom with parchment (baking) paper.

To make the cake: Sift the flour, the cocoa powder, 1 cup (200 g) of the sugar, the five-spice powder, cinnamon, baking powder, and salt into a large bowl. Use a large spoon to make

(continued)

an indentation in the center of the flour mixture and add the oil, egg yolks, water, and vanilla. Using an electric mixer on medium speed, beat the mixture until smooth and thick, about 3 minutes. Stop the mixer and scrape the sides of the bowl as needed. Set aside.

In a clean large bowl, using clean beaters, beat the egg whites and cream of tartar on low speed until the whites are foamy and the cream of tartar dissolves. On medium speed, beat the egg whites until they look shiny and smooth and the movement of the beaters forms lines in the mixture. When you stop the mixer and lift the beaters, the beaten whites should cling to them. On high speed, slowly beat in the remaining ½ cup (100 g) sugar, 1 tbsp at a time, then beat for 1 minute until the whites form firm glossy peaks. Use a rubber spatula to fold the milk chocolate into the reserved egg yolk mixture. Stir about one-third of the beaten whites into the yolk mixture, then fold in the remaining whites until no white streaks remain. Scrape the batter into the tube pan and gently smooth the top.

Bake until the top feels firm when lightly touched and any small cracks look dry, about 1 hour and 10 minutes. Invert the pan onto a narrow-necked bottle (a full wine bottle is stable and works well) and let cool for 1 hour. Run a thin knife around the sides and center tube to loosen the cake. Invert the cake onto a wire rack so it is bottom up. Cool the cake thoroughly on the wire rack.

To make the glaze: In a medium saucepan, heat the cream and corn (golden) syrup over low heat until the cream is hot. Do not let the mixture boil. Remove the pan from the heat, add the milk chocolate, and let it sit in the hot cream mixture for about 30 seconds to soften. Whisk the glaze until the chocolate is melted and smooth. Stir in the vanilla. Use a thin metal spatula to spread the glaze over the top of the cake, letting it drip down the sides. Let the glaze firm for about 1 hour.

Put the five-spice powder in a small strainer and dust it lightly and evenly over the glaze. Use a spoon to lay one chocolate strip on the glaze, then lay another strip across it. Arrange five more pairs of strips over the top of the cake. Slip a large metal spatula under the cake and slide it onto a serving plate. The cooled cake is sturdy and easy to move. Use a serrated knife to cut the cake into slices.

The cake can be covered and stored at room temperature for up to 3 days.

chocolate-hazelnut sour cream cake

MAKES 12 SERVINGS

Finely ground hazelnuts, sugar, and chocolate give this cake a crunchy texture. Characteristic of sour cream cakes, it is supermoist and suits any occasion. Serve it with whipped cream for a special dinner, or simply cut it into slices for a lunch or tea party. Not characteristic of sour cream cakes is that it is a dark chocolate cake with bits of chocolate throughout. That turns a good idea into a great one.

✳ Mixing time 15 minutes

✳ Baking 350°F (180°C/gas mark 4) for about 1 hour and 5 minutes

---

6 OZ (170 G) SEMISWEET (PLAIN) CHOCOLATE, CHOPPED

¾ CUP (120 G) HAZELNUTS (FILBERTS), PEELED, TOASTED, AND CHOPPED (SEE PAGE 17)

2½ CUPS (500 G) GRANULATED SUGAR

2½ TSP GROUND CINNAMON

2 CUPS (225 G) CAKE (SOFT-WHEAT) FLOUR

¾ CUP (70 G) UNSWEETENED DUTCH-PROCESS COCOA POWDER

¾ TSP BAKING POWDER

¾ TSP BAKING SODA (BICARBONATE OF SODA)

½ TSP SALT

3 LARGE EGGS

1 CUP (240 ML) CANOLA OR CORN OIL

2 TSP VANILLA EXTRACT (ESSENCE)

1 CUP (225 G) SOUR CREAM

POWDERED (ICING) SUGAR FOR DUSTING

Position a rack in the middle of the oven. Preheat the oven to 350°F (180°C/gas mark 4). Butter the bottom, sides, and center tube of a 9½- or 10-in (24- or 25-cm) fixed-bottom tube pan with sides at least 3¾ in (9.5 cm) high. Line the bottom with parchment (baking) paper and butter the paper.

Process the chocolate, hazelnuts, ½ cup (100 g) of the granulated sugar, and 1 teaspoon of the cinnamon in a food processor until the nuts and chocolate are finely ground. Set aside.

Sift the flour, cocoa powder, the remaining 1½ teaspoons cinnamon, the baking powder, baking soda (bicarbonate of soda), and salt into a medium bowl and set aside.

In a large bowl, using an electric mixer on medium speed, beat the eggs and the remaining 2 cups (400 g) granulated sugar until fluffy, thick, and lightened in color, about 2 minutes. Stop the mixer and scrape the sides of the bowl as needed. On low speed, mix in the oil and vanilla until blended. Mix in the flour mixture just to incorporate it. Mix in the sour cream until no white streaks remain. Set aside ¼ cup (60 ml) of the hazelnut mixture. Use a rubber spatula to stir the remaining hazelnut mixture into the batter just to distribute it. Scrape the batter into the prepared pan and gently smooth the top. Sprinkle the reserved hazelnut mixture over the batter.

Bake until a toothpick inserted in the center comes out clean or with just a few moist crumbs clinging to it, about 1 hour and 5 minutes. Cool the cake in the pan on a wire rack for 15 minutes. Run a thin knife around the sides and center tube to loosen the cake. Invert the cake onto the rack. Carefully remove and discard the paper. Invert the cake onto another wire rack so that it is top up. Cool completely. Lightly dust the cake with powdered (icing) sugar. Transfer the cake to a serving plate. Use a large knife to cut the cake into slices.

The cake can be covered and stored at room temperature for up to 3 days.

chocolate-swirl chocolate pound cake

You know that something good is coming when each slice of this cake displays a very dark interior with thin swirls of even darker chocolate. And then there is the aroma. When a friend, Dawn Ryan, tested the cake for me, she wrote, "This cake comes with an intoxicating aroma of chocolate when it bakes and for *hours* after." Cocoa powder plus melted chocolate produces the rich, dark chocolate color, and the additional melted chocolate swirled into the batter provides the ripples of pure chocolate.

This large cake bakes in a tube pan and is a good choice to take to a large gathering like a family reunion. The batter could also be baked in two loaf pans, to make one cake for serving now and another for later. Since the cake has a small quantity of leavening, it is important to develop the cake's structure by thoroughly beating the butter and sugar and again when adding the eggs.

❋ Mixing time 15 minutes

❋ Baking 325°F (165°C/gas mark 3) for about 1 hour and 10 minutes

---

3 OZ (85 G) UNSWEETENED CHOCOLATE, CHOPPED

6 OZ (170 G) SEMISWEET (PLAIN) CHOCOLATE, CHOPPED

2¾ CUPS (355 G) UNBLEACHED ALL-PURPOSE (PLAIN) FLOUR

½ CUP (45 G) UNSWEETENED DUTCH-PROCESS COCOA POWDER

½ TSP BAKING POWDER

½ TSP BAKING SODA (BICARBONATE OF SODA)

½ TSP SALT

1½ CUPS (340 G) UNSALTED BUTTER, AT ROOM TEMPERATURE

1½ CUPS (300 G) GRANULATED SUGAR

1½ CUPS (300 G) PACKED LIGHT BROWN SUGAR

6 LARGE EGGS, AT ROOM TEMPERATURE FOR 1 HOUR

2 TSP VANILLA EXTRACT (ESSENCE)

1 CUP (225 G) SOUR CREAM

POWDERED (ICING) SUGAR FOR DUSTING

Position a rack in the middle of the oven. Preheat the oven to 325°F (165°C/gas mark 3). Butter the bottom, sides, and center tube of a 9½- or 10-in (24- or 25-cm) fixed-bottom tube pan with sides at least 3¾ in (9.5 cm) high. Line the bottom with parchment (baking) paper and butter the paper.

Put the unsweetened chocolate in a heatproof bowl (or the top of a double boiler) and place it over, but not touching, barely simmering water in a saucepan (or the bottom of the double boiler). Stir until the chocolate is melted and smooth. Remove from over the water and set aside to cool slightly. In another bowl, melt the semisweet (plain) chocolate over the barely simmering water and set aside to cool slightly.

Sift the flour, cocoa powder, baking powder, baking soda (bicarbonate of soda) and salt into a medium bowl and set aside. In a large bowl, using an electric mixer on medium speed, beat the butter and granulated and brown sugars until fluffy and smooth, about 3 minutes. Stop the mixer and scrape the sides of the bowl as needed. Crack the eggs into a small bowl and use a fork to beat them lightly. Add the eggs in three additions, mixing for about 1 minute until each addition is blended into the butter mixture, and mixing in the vanilla with the last addition. Beat for 1 minute more. On low speed, mix in the unsweetened chocolate. Mix in the sour cream until no white streaks remain. Mix in the flour mixture just until it is incorporated and the batter is smooth.

Pour about two-thirds of the batter into the prepared pan. Leaving a 1-in (2.5-cm) plain edge around the outside of the pan and the tube, spoon about half of the semisweet (plain) chocolate over the batter. Swirl once with a knife. Spoon the remaining chocolate over the remaining one-third batter in the bowl and swirl gently to streak it through the batter, but not blend it into the batter. Pour the batter into the pan and use a thin metal spatula to spread it evenly.

Bake until the top feels firm when lightly touched and a toothpick inserted in the center comes out clean, about 1 hour and 10 minutes. Cool the cake in the pan on a wire rack for about 1½ hours. Run a thin knife around the sides and center tube to loosen the cake. Invert the cake onto the rack.

Carefully remove and discard the parchment (baking) paper. Invert a serving platter on the cake and turn the cake so that it is top up. Dust lightly with powdered (icing) sugar, and use a large knife to cut the cake into slices.

The cake can be covered and stored at room temperature for up to 3 days.

Choices: This cake can be baked in two 9-by-5-by-3-in (23-by-12-by-7.5-cm) loaf pans. Divide the batter and melted chocolate for swirling evenly between the pans. The cakes will need to bake for about 1 hour, but should be checked after 55 minutes.

banana-butterscotch upside-down chocolate cake

Fresh bananas make an always-in-season fruit topping for this upside-down chocolate cake. The bananas become infused with the sauce and turn a butterscotch color as the cake bakes. Bananas that are ripe but firm will hold their shape nicely during baking.

* Mixing time 10 minutes
* Baking 350°F (180°C/gas mark 4) for about 35 minutes

---

butterscotch sauce

- ½ CUP (120 ML) HEAVY (DOUBLE) CREAM
- ¼ CUP (55 G) UNSALTED BUTTER, AT ROOM TEMPERATURE
- ½ CUP (100 G) PACKED DARK BROWN SUGAR
- 2 TBSP GRANULATED SUGAR
- ¼ TSP SALT
- ¼ CUP (60 ML) LIGHT (GOLDEN) CORN SYRUP
- 3 LARGE RIPE BUT FIRM BANANAS, CUT INTO ½-IN (12-MM) SLICES

cake

- 1 CUP (130 G) CAKE (SOFT-WHEAT) FLOUR
- ⅓ CUP (30 G) UNSWEETENED DUTCH-PROCESS COCOA POWDER
- ½ TSP BAKING SODA (BICARBONATE OF SODA)
- ¼ TSP SALT
- 6 TBSP (85 G) UNSALTED BUTTER, AT ROOM TEMPERATURE
- ½ CUP (100 G) GRANULATED SUGAR
- ½ CUP (100 G) PACKED DARK BROWN SUGAR
- 2 LARGE EGGS
- 1 TSP VANILLA EXTRACT (ESSENCE)
- ⅔ CUP (165 ML) BUTTERMILK

  BANANA OR VANILLA ICE CREAM FOR SERVING (OPTIONAL)

Position a rack in the middle of the oven. Preheat the oven to 350°F (180°C/gas mark 4). Butter a 9-in (23-cm) square baking pan with sides 2 in (5 cm) high. Line with a piece of aluminum foil long enough to extend over opposite sides of the pan.

To make the butterscotch sauce: In a medium saucepan, cook the cream, butter, brown and granulated sugars, salt, and corn (golden) syrup over low heat, stirring occasionally, until the butter and sugars are melted. Increase the heat to medium-high, bring the sauce to a boil, and boil, stirring constantly, for 1 minute. Pour the sauce into the prepared pan, tilting the pan if necessary to spread it evenly. Arrange the banana slices in rows over the sauce, placing them close together. Set aside.

To make the cake: Sift the flour, cocoa powder, baking soda (bicarbonate of soda), and salt into a medium bowl and set aside. In a large bowl, using an electric mixer on medium speed, beat the butter and granulated and brown sugars until smoothly blended, about 2 minutes. Stop the mixer and scrape the sides of the bowl as needed. Add the eggs one at a time, beating until each is blended smoothly into the batter and the batter looks creamy, about 2 minutes. Mix in the vanilla. On low speed, add half of the flour mixture, mixing just to incorporate it. Mix in the buttermilk to blend it into the batter. Mix in the remaining flour mixture until it is incorporated and the batter is smooth. Scrape the batter evenly over the bananas. Gently smooth the top.

Bake just until the top feels firm when lightly touched and a toothpick inserted in the center of the cake, but not the bananas, comes out clean, about 35 minutes. Cool the cake in the pan on a wire rack for 10 minutes. Invert the cake onto the rack. Carefully remove and discard the foil. If any bananas stick to the foil, replace them on the cake. Cool the cake thoroughly on the wire rack for about 1 hour. Transfer the cake to a serving plate. Use a large knife to cut the cake into squares. Serve with ice cream, if desired.

The cake can be covered and stored at room temperature overnight.

chocolate whiskey cake

This cake is a "keeper." It has the characteristic of improving in flavor after a day or two. Whiskey helps preserve the cake, and dates soaked in the whiskey keep the cake quite moist. The unique cream cheese and whiskey frosting has the texture of a thick glaze. Irish whiskey, scotch, or bourbon make the best liquor choices. If the Bundt pan is carefully oiled and evenly floured, the baked cake will release easily.

☀ Mixing time 15 minutes

☀ Baking 350°F (180°C/gas mark 4) for about 1 hour and 5 minutes

cake

1½ CUPS (90 G) PITTED DATES, CUT INTO ¾-IN (2-CM) PIECES

¾ CUP (180 ML) WHISKEY

2¼ CUPS (285 G) UNBLEACHED ALL-PURPOSE (PLAIN) FLOUR

½ CUP (45 G) UNSWEETENED DUTCH-PROCESS COCOA POWDER

1 TSP GROUND CINNAMON

2 TSP BAKING POWDER

¾ TSP BAKING SODA (BICARBONATE OF SODA)

½ TSP SALT

3 LARGE EGGS

2 CUPS (400 G) PACKED LIGHT BROWN SUGAR

1 CUP (240 ML) CANOLA OR CORN OIL

2 TSP VANILLA EXTRACT (ESSENCE)

1 CUP (115 G) TOASTED WALNUTS (SEE PAGE 17), FINELY CHOPPED

glaze

2 OZ (55 G) CREAM CHEESE, SOFTENED

¼ CUP (55 G) UNSALTED BUTTER, MELTED

⅔ CUP (70 G) POWDERED (ICING) SUGAR

1 TBSP WHISKEY

2 TO 3 TSP WATER

½ CUP (55 G) TOASTED WALNUTS (SEE PAGE 17), COARSELY CHOPPED

Position a rack in the middle of the oven. Preheat the oven to 350°F (180°C/gas mark 4). Oil a Bundt pan, with a capacity of 3 qt (2.8 L), then sprinkle flour lightly inside the pan and tilt the pan to coat it evenly. Tap out and discard any loose flour.

To make the cake: Put the dates in a small bowl, pour the whiskey over them, and stir to coat. Let sit for 15 minutes, or cover and let sit overnight.

Sift the flour, cocoa powder, cinnamon, baking powder, baking soda (bicarbonate of soda), and salt into a medium bowl and set aside. In a large bowl, using an electric mixer on medium speed, beat the eggs and brown sugar until fluffy, thick, and lightened in color, about 2 minutes. On low speed, mix in the oil and vanilla until blended. Mix in the dates and their soaking whiskey. Mix in the flour mixture just to incorporate it. Mix in the walnuts. Scrape the batter into the prepared pan.

Bake until a toothpick inserted in the center comes out clean or with just a few moist crumbs clinging to it, about 1 hour and 5 minutes. Cool the cake in the pan on a wire rack for 15 minutes. Use a small, sharp knife to loosen the cake from the edges and center tube of the pan. Invert the cake onto the wire rack, tapping the bottom of the pan several times if it does not release immediately. Cool the cake completely.

To make the glaze: In a large bowl, using an electric mixer on medium speed, beat the cream cheese, butter, and powdered (icing) sugar until smoothly blended. On low speed, mix in the whiskey and the water, 1 tsp at a time, until a smooth, pourable glaze forms.

Use a small spoon to drizzle the glaze over the top of the cake, letting it drip down the sides. Let the glaze set for 10 minutes. Sprinkle the walnuts over the top. The glaze will remain soft. Transfer the cake to a serving plate. Use a large knife to cut the cake into slices.

The cake can be carefully covered and refrigerated for up to 5 days. Bring to room temperature to serve.

chocolate-apricot pudding cake with chocolate toffee sauce

Many years ago, my husband and I were lucky enough to stay at Sharrow Bay Country House Hotel in the England's Lake District. That was where I first tasted the sticky toffee pudding that was served every day at lunch. The original owners, Brian Sack and Francis Colson, wanted guests to feel as if they were visiting a country house, not a hotel. This philosophy included writing out their treasured recipe for the pudding and sharing it with me. My fondness for this cake has only grown over the years, and I have come up with my own variations. My newest is this dark chocolate and apricot cake that has a bit of chocolate in the traditional toffee sauce. The pudding has a pleasing dense texture, and the tartness of the dried apricots contrasts nicely with the sweet sauce.

The English call their dessert course *pudding*, and this is not a pudding as we would think of one, but a supermoist cake. The toffee sauce bakes on top of the cake and is also served with the cake. The sauce can be made up to one week ahead, covered, and refrigerated. Before using it, warm it over low heat, stirring to blend it smoothly.

☀ Mixing time 25 minutes for cake and sauce

☀ Baking 350°F (180°C/gas mark 4) for about 45 minutes and
250°F (120°C/gas mark ½) for about 20 minutes

---

sauce

2   CUPS (480 ML) HEAVY (DOUBLE) CREAM

1½ CUPS (300 G) PACKED DARK BROWN SUGAR

1   OZ (30 G) UNSWEETENED CHOCOLATE, CHOPPED

1   TSP VANILLA EXTRACT (ESSENCE)

cake

1   CUP (170 G) DRIED APRICOTS

1   CUP (240 ML) WATER

2   OZ (60 G) UNSWEETENED CHOCOLATE, CHOPPED

1   CUP (130 G) UNBLEACHED ALL-PURPOSE (PLAIN) FLOUR

⅓ CUP (30 G) UNSWEETENED DUTCH-PROCESS COCOA POWDER

1   TSP BAKING POWDER

½ TSP SALT

¼ CUP (55 G) UNSALTED BUTTER, AT ROOM TEMPERATURE

1   CUP (200 G) GRANULATED SUGAR

2   LARGE EGGS

1   TSP VANILLA EXTRACT (ESSENCE)

1   TSP BAKING SODA (BICARBONATE OF SODA)

1   CUP (240 ML) CRÈME FRAÎCHE OR HEAVY (DOUBLE) CREAM

(continued)

To make the sauce: In a medium saucepan, heat the cream and brown sugar over medium-low heat, stirring occasionally, until the sugar dissolves. Increase the heat to medium-high and bring the sauce to a simmer. Stirring often and adjusting the heat as necessary, simmer the sauce until reduced and thickened slightly, about 10 minutes. Remove from the heat and stir in the chocolate, stirring gently to help it melt evenly. Stir in the vanilla. You will have about 2½ cups (600 ml) toffee sauce. Set aside.

Position a rack in the middle of the oven. Preheat the oven to 350°F (180°C/gas mark 4). Butter a 9-by-5-by-3-in (23-by-12-by-7.5-cm) loaf pan or a loaf pan with a capacity of 6 to 8 cups (1.4 to 2 L). Line the bottom with parchment (baking) paper and butter the paper.

To make the cake: Put the apricots and water in a small saucepan and bring to a boil. Remove from the heat and let cool for at least 5 minutes or up to 2 hours. In a food processor, process the apricots, including any remaining water, to a coarse puree. Set aside.

Put the chocolate in a heatproof bowl (or the top of a double boiler) and place it over, but not touching, barely simmering water in a saucepan (or the bottom of the double boiler). Stir until the chocolate is melted and smooth. Remove from over the water and set aside to cool slightly.

Sift the flour, cocoa powder, baking powder, and salt into a medium bowl. Set aside. In a large bowl, using an electric mixer on medium speed, beat the butter and granulated sugar until smoothly blended, about 1 minute. Stop the mixer and scrape the sides of the bowl as needed. Add the eggs and vanilla and mix until smoothly blended, about 2 minutes. Mix in the melted chocolate until it is blended into the batter. On low speed, add the flour mixture, mixing just until it is incorporated. Press any lumps out of the baking soda (bicarbonate of soda) and gently stir it into the apricots. Use a large spoon to gently mix the apricots into the batter. Scrape the batter into the prepared pan.

Bake until the top feels firm when gently touched and a toothpick inserted in the center comes out clean, about 45 minutes. Decrease the oven temperature to 250°F (120°C/gas mark ½). Remove the pan from the oven and pour ½ cup (120 ml) of the warm toffee sauce over the cake, tilting the pan gently to spread it evenly. Bake for an additional 20 minutes.

Let the cake cool completely in the pan on a wire rack, about 1 hour. Use a small, sharp knife to loosen the cake from the sides of the pan, and invert the cake onto a flat plate. Carefully remove and discard the paper. Invert a serving plate on the cake and turn the cake so that it is top up. The cake can be covered and stored at room temperature for up to 2 days.

To serve, warm the remaining toffee sauce over low heat, if necessary. Cut the cake into eight slices, then cut each slice in half. Arrange two half slices in each individual shallow serving bowl. Pour the warm sauce over each serving and garnish with a generous spoonful of crème fraîche.

pear and chocolate crumb cake

When I bake a cake like this in a big rectangular pan, I start cutting small pieces as soon as the cake comes out of the oven. After all, I have to see how it tastes when the chocolate is warm and soft, then when the cake starts to cool and the crumbs begin to get crisp, and then when the pears cool a bit and the chocolate starts to firm up. It is always a big surprise when I see how much I have eaten. Luckily, this is a big cake, and there is plenty for others, too.

❊ Mixing time 15 minutes

❊ Baking 325°F (165°C/gas mark 3) for about 55 minutes

topping

1 CUP (130 G) UNBLEACHED ALL-PURPOSE (PLAIN) FLOUR

1 CUP (200 G) PACKED LIGHT BROWN SUGAR

2 TBSP UNSWEETENED DUTCH-PROCESS COCOA POWDER, SIFTED

1 TSP GROUND CINNAMON

½ CUP (115 G) COLD UNSALTED BUTTER, CUT INTO PIECES

6 OZ (170 G) SEMISWEET (PLAIN) CHOCOLATE, COARSELY CHOPPED

cake

2½ CUPS (320 G) UNBLEACHED ALL-PURPOSE (PLAIN) FLOUR

1 TSP BAKING POWDER

¾ TSP BAKING SODA (BICARBONATE OF SODA)

1 TSP GROUND CINNAMON

½ TSP SALT

¾ CUP (170 G) UNSALTED BUTTER, AT ROOM TEMPERATURE, CUT INTO PIECES

2 CUPS (400 G) GRANULATED SUGAR

4 LARGE EGGS

1 TSP VANILLA EXTRACT (ESSENCE)

1 CUP (225 G) SOUR CREAM

8 OZ (225 G) SEMISWEET (PLAIN) CHOCOLATE BARS, BROKEN INTO PIECES AT LEAST 1 IN (2.5 CM)

2 PEARS, PEELED, CORED, AND CUT INTO PIECES ABOUT ¾ IN (2 CM)

POWDERED (ICING) SUGAR FOR DUSTING

Position a rack in the middle of the oven. Preheat the oven to 325°F (165°C/gas mark 3). Butter a 13-by-9-by-2-in (33-by-23-by-5-cm) baking pan.

To make the topping: In a large bowl, using an electric mixer on medium speed, beat the flour, brown sugar, cocoa powder, and cinnamon to blend. Add the butter and mix until crumbs form. The largest butter pieces will be about ¼ in (6 mm), and you will still see some loose flour. Stir in the chopped chocolate. Set aside.

To make the cake: Sift the flour, baking powder, baking soda (bicarbonate of soda), cinnamon, and salt into a medium bowl. Set aside. In a large bowl, using an electric mixer on medium speed, beat the butter and sugar until smoothly blended, about 2 minutes. Stop the mixer and scrape the sides of the bowl as needed. Beat in the eggs two at a time, incorporating the first addition before adding the second. Beat in

(continued)

the vanilla with the second addition of eggs, then beat for 1 minute. The mixture may look slightly curdled. On low speed, add half of the flour mixture, mixing just until it is incorporated. Mix in the sour cream and then the remaining flour mixture just until it is incorporated. Scrape half of the batter into the prepared pan. Place the broken chocolate bars on the batter to form a mostly solid layer of chocolate. Scrape the remaining batter over the chocolate, spreading it evenly. Place the pears evenly on the batter. Spoon the topping evenly over the pears.

Bake until the center feels firm when lightly touched and a toothpick inserted in the center comes out clean or with a few moist crumbs clinging to it, about 55 minutes. The melted chocolate might cling to the toothpick, but the cake should not.

Cool the cake completely in the pan on a wire rack, about 1½ hours. Dust the top with powdered (icing) sugar. Cut into squares and serve.

The cake can be covered and stored at room temperature for up to 3 days.

chocolate pavlova

Pavlova territory is in Australia and New Zealand. Each country claims to have originated the dessert—a large meringue that is crisp on the outside and has a marshmallow consistency on the inside. The meringue is heaped with whipped cream and fresh berries or fruit. In this version, chocolate meringue is lined with chocolate and then filled with whipped cream and strawberries. When my daughter-in-law Kate, who bakes a lot, tested this cake for me, Max, my five-year-old grandson, said, "Mommy, this is the best cake you ever made. I'm going to make it every night when I grow up!"

☀ Mixing time 15 minutes for cake and filling

☀ Baking 250°F (120°C/gas mark ½) for 1 hour and 30 minutes

---

1   **TBSP POWDERED (ICING) SUGAR FOR BAKING SHEET**

cake

3   **TBSP UNSWEETENED DUTCH-PROCESS COCOA POWDER**

1½ **TSP CORNSTARCH (CORNFLOUR)**

4   **LARGE EGG WHITES, AT ROOM TEMPERATURE**

¼   **TSP CREAM OF TARTAR**

1   **CUP (200 G) GRANULATED SUGAR**

1   **TSP VINEGAR**

filling

3   **OZ (85 G) SEMISWEET (PLAIN) CHOCOLATE, CHOPPED**

1½ **CUPS (360 ML) COLD HEAVY (DOUBLE) CREAM**

3   **TBSP POWDERED (ICING) SUGAR**

1   **TSP VANILLA EXTRACT (ESSENCE)**

2   **CUPS (225 G) HULLED AND HALVED STRAWBERRIES**

4   **LARGE STRAWBERRIES WITH STEMS (OPTIONAL)**

½   **CUP (120 ML) GANACHE (PAGE 26), COOLED UNTIL JUST THICK ENOUGH TO CLING TO THE STRAWBERRIES (OPTIONAL)**

Position a rack in the middle of the oven. Preheat the oven to 250°F (120°C/gas mark ½). Line a baking sheet (tray) with parchment (baking) paper. Butter the paper and sift the 1 tbsp powdered (icing) sugar evenly over the butter. Use the tip of a small knife to mark a 9-in (23-cm) circle in the sugar.

To make the cake: Sift the cocoa powder and cornstarch (cornflour) into a small bowl. In a clean large bowl, using an electric mixer on low speed, beat the egg whites and cream of tartar until the whites are foamy and the cream of tartar dissolves. On medium speed, beat the egg whites until they look shiny and smooth and the movement of the beaters forms lines in the mixture. When you stop the mixer and lift the beaters,

the beaten whites should cling to them. Slowly beat in the granulated sugar, 2 tbsp at a time, then beat for 1 minute. On low speed, mix in the cocoa mixture by sprinkling it over the egg white mixture. Mix in the vinegar (you will not taste this when the meringue is baked).

Use a thin metal spatula to spread the meringue mixture inside the marked circle. Then use the spatula to form a 6-in (15-cm) well in the center; the edges of the well will be higher than the center of the meringue.

Bake until the meringue feels crisp and dry when lightly touched, about 1 hour. Turn off the oven and leave the

(continued)

meringue in the oven for 30 minutes. Remove the baking sheet from the oven and cool the meringue completely on the baking sheet for about 45 minutes.

To make the filling: Put the chocolate in a heatproof bowl (or the top of a double boiler) and place it over, but not touching, barely simmering water in a saucepan (or the bottom of the double boiler). Stir until the chocolate is melted and smooth. Spoon the chocolate over the well in the center of the baked meringue, and use the back of the spoon to gently spread the chocolate evenly. Let sit until the chocolate is firm, about 30 minutes. Or, refrigerate for about 10 minutes to firm the chocolate. Use a wide spatula to slide the meringue onto a serving plate.

In a large bowl, using an electric mixer on medium-high speed, beat the cream, powdered (icing) sugar, and vanilla until firm peaks form. Spoon the whipped cream over the chocolate-lined well, mounding it toward the center. It is fine if some spills onto the raised edge of the meringue. Arrange the halved strawberries, cut-side down, over the whipped cream. If desired, hold each of the 4 large strawberries by the stem and dip the bottom half into the ganache; arrange them in the center of the meringue.

Serve, or cover and refrigerate for up to 3 hours. Use a large, sharp knife to cut the pavlova or a large spoon to spoon out portions.

brandied chocolate cheesecake with chocolate-dipped figs

Cheesecakes always look sophisticated and as if they took a lot of time to prepare, and two-tone cheesecakes look even more spectacular and complicated. But here's a secret: Cheesecakes are easily and quickly mixed, and this one is no exception. In this recipe, one batch of batter is flavored two different ways, and the top segment is made by simply pouring the batter over the partially baked bottom portion. A bonus is that these types of cheesecakes hardly ever develop cracks on top as they cool.

Be sure to soften the cream cheese thoroughly so it mixes smoothly into the batter. A quick method for softening cream cheese is to let the wrapped packages sit in a sunny window, just until the cream cheese feels soft when pressed with a finger.

✳ Mixing time 25 minutes for crust, filling, and ganache

✳ Baking 325°F (165°C/gas mark 3) for 8 minutes for crust and about 1 hour and 5 minutes for cheesecake

---

crust

1½ CUPS (150 G) CHOCOLATE COOKIE CRUMBS

½ CUP (85 G) MINIATURE SEMISWEET (PLAIN) CHOCOLATE CHIPS

5 TBSP (70 G) UNSALTED BUTTER, MELTED

filling

4 OR 5 LARGE DRIED CALIMYRA FIGS, CUT INTO PIECES ½ IN (12 MM) OR LESS

¼ CUP (60 ML) BRANDY PLUS 3 TBSP

6 OZ (170 G) SEMISWEET (PLAIN) CHOCOLATE, CHOPPED

2 LB (910 G) CREAM CHEESE, AT ROOM TEMPERATURE

1¼ CUPS (250 G) SUGAR

2 TBSP UNBLEACHED ALL-PURPOSE (PLAIN) FLOUR

4 LARGE EGGS, LIGHTLY BEATEN AND AT ROOM TEMPERATURE

2 TBSP HEAVY (DOUBLE) CREAM

2 TSP VANILLA EXTRACT (ESSENCE)

½ CUP (120 ML) GANACHE (PAGE 26), COOLED UNTIL THICKENED BUT POURABLE

12 LARGE DRIED CALIMYRA FIGS

Position a rack in the middle of the oven. Preheat the oven to 325°F (165°C/gas mark 3). Butter a 9-in (23-cm) springform pan with sides 2¾ in (7 cm) high. Wrap the outside of the pan with a large piece of heavy aluminum foil. Have ready a large baking pan with sides at least 2 in (5 cm) high that is large enough to hold the springform pan.

(continued)

To make the crust: In a large bowl, stir the cookie crumbs and chocolate chips together. Mix in the melted butter to moisten the crumbs evenly. Scrape the crumb mixture into the prepared pan, and using your fingers or the back of a spoon, press the crumb mixture evenly over the bottom and 1 in (2.5 cm) up the sides. Be careful not to make the crust too thick where the bottom meets the sides. Bake for 8 minutes. Set aside to cool while you mix the filling.

To make the filling: Put the fig pieces in a small bowl and stir in the 3 tbsp brandy. Let sit for at least 1 hour, or cover and refrigerate overnight.

Put the semisweet (plain) chocolate in a heatproof bowl (or the top of a double boiler) and place it over, but not touching, barely simmering water in a saucepan (or the bottom of the double boiler). Stir until the chocolate is melted and smooth. Remove from over the water and set aside to cool slightly.

In a large bowl, using an electric mixer on low speed, beat the cream cheese and sugar just until smoothly blended. Mix in the flour. Beat in the eggs in two additions just to blend them in smoothly. Mix in the ¼ cup (60 ml) brandy, cream, and vanilla. Pour 2 cups (480 ml) of the batter into a medium bowl and set aside; this will be used for the top layer. Mix the melted chocolate into the remaining batter. Scrape the batter into the baked crust.

Put the springform pan in the large baking pan and place in the preheated oven. Pour hot water in the large pan to reach 1-in (2.5 cm) up the sides of the springform pan. Bake for 45 minutes. Carefully slide the oven rack out several inches. Slowly pour the reserved batter around the inside edge of the springform pan. The batter will flow evenly toward the center and cover the cheesecake. Spoon the brandy-soaked figs evenly over the batter. Bake for 20 minutes. Give the cheesecake a gentle shake; when it is done, the top should look firm.

Cool the cheesecake, covered loosely with paper towels (absorbent paper), in its water bath for 1 hour. Carefully remove the cheesecake from the water bath. Remove the paper towels (absorbent paper) and foil wrapping from the pan, and let the cake sit until it feels cool to the touch, about 1 hour. Cover the cheesecake with plastic wrap (cling film) and chill thoroughly in the refrigerator for at least 6 hours or up to overnight. The cheesecake becomes firm when chilled. It can be refrigerated for up to 4 days before the fig topping is added.

Use a small knife to loosen the cheesecake from the sides of the pan and remove the sides. Put the ganache in a small bowl. Holding each fig by the stem, dip it into the ganache to cover about three-fourths of the fig. Put the figs on a wire rack to let the ganache firm, about 30 minutes. Arrange the figs in a border around the top of the cheesecake. Let the cheesecake sit at room temperature for 1 to 2 hours before serving. Use a large, sharp knife to cut the cheesecake, carefully wiping it clean after cutting each slice. Each slice will include a chocolate-dipped fig.

chocolate layer cakes

The cakes in this chapter have one thing in common: they have at least two layers that are filled and frosted. From then on, anything goes. A chocolate-and-orange-frosted cake has the traditional two layers of frosting and filling. The Salted Caramel and Pecan Chocolate Cake, a large-diameter cake, is filled and topped with salted caramel sauce and sweet and salty pecans. For the Chocolate Zebra Cake, a thin sheet of chocolate cake is cut into four equal pieces to create a four-layer black-and-white cake. For several cakes, two layers are split into four to hold lots of filling and frosting. The Ginger-Chocolate Cake Roll is rolled up like a sponge cake around a filling. These are just some of the many forms that layer cakes can take.

chocolate ganache cake

Dark chocolate cake, creamy filling, and a fudge glaze that covers it all might sound complicated. In reality, you need only one batch of ganache. Some is whisked to make the filling, and the remainder is used without being whipped to make the glaze.

* Mixing time 15 minutes for cake and ganache
* Baking 350°F (180°C/gas mark 4) for about 45 minutes

ONE 10-IN (25-CM) DEVIL'S FOOD CAKE LAYER (PAGE 28), BAKED AND COOLED

4   CUPS (960 ML) GANACHE (PAGE 26)

Transfer the cake layer to a serving plate so that it is top up. Tuck wax (greaseproof) paper strips 1 in (2.5 cm) or so under the cake all the way around to keep the plate clean.

Put 2½ cups (600 ml) of the ganache in a large bowl. Let cool at room temperature until it thickens to a firm texture, 1 to 2 hours. Or, cover and refrigerate the ganache until the edges are firm, about 1 hour.

Use a long serrated knife to cut the cake layer horizontally into two even layers. Carefully slip the removable bottom of a tart pan or springform pan between the layers, lift the top layer, and set it aside. Use a whisk to beat the thickened ganache for about 30 seconds until the color lightens from a dark brown to a medium brown (see page 26). The texture will change from fudgelike to creamlike. Immediately use a thin metal spatula to spread all of the filling over the bottom cake layer, spreading it to the edges.

Carefully slide the top of the cake onto the filling, centering it over the bottom layer. If any filling spills onto the sides (it would be a small quantity), use the spatula to spread it on the sides of the cake. If necessary, briefly warm the remaining 1½ cups (360 ml) ganache in a medium saucepan over low heat just until it is pourable but thick enough to cling to the cake. Use a clean spatula to spread the ganache over the top and sides of the cake. Remove the paper strips and discard them.

Use a large, sharp knife to cut the cake, carefully wiping it clean after each slice.

The cake can be covered and refrigerated for up to 2 days. Let it sit at room temperature for about 45 minutes before serving.

mocha whipped cream truffle cake

Chocolate and coffee have the power to intensify the flavor of each other. This cake uses the combination to fill and frost four chocolate cake layers with alternating layers of chocolate ganache and coffee whipped cream.

✳ Mixing time 30 minutes for cake, filling, and ganache
✳ Baking 350°F (180°C/gas mark 4) for about 35 minutes

coffee syrup

½ CUP (120 ML) HOT STRONG COFFEE

¼ CUP (50 G) GRANULATED SUGAR

coffee whipped cream

2 CUPS (480 ML) COLD HEAVY (DOUBLE) CREAM

½ CUP (50 G) POWDERED (ICING) SUGAR

4 TSP INSTANT COFFEE GRANULES

1 TSP VANILLA EXTRACT (ESSENCE)

TWO 9-IN (23-CM) DEVIL'S FOOD CAKE LAYERS (PAGE 28), BAKED AND COOLED

2 CUPS (480 ML) GANACHE (PAGE 26), COOLED AND AT SPREADING CONSISTENCY

CHOCOLATE SHARDS (SEE PAGE 13)

To make the coffee syrup: In a small bowl, stir the coffee and sugar together to dissolve the sugar. Set aside.

To make the coffee whipped cream: In a large bowl, using an electric mixer on medium-high speed, beat the cream, powdered (icing) sugar, instant coffee, and vanilla until firm peaks form. The coffee will dissolve as the cream whips.

Transfer one of the cake layers to a serving plate so that it is top up. Tuck wax (greaseproof) paper strips 1 in (2.5 cm) or so under the cake all the way around to keep the plate clean.

Use a long serrated knife to cut the cake layer horizontally into two even layers. Carefully slip the removable bottom of a tart pan or springform pan between the layers, lift the top layer, and set it aside. Use a pastry brush to lightly brush the top of each layer with the coffee syrup. Pour 1 cup (240 ml) of the ganache in the center of the bottom layer and use a small spatula to spread it evenly over the cake. Carefully slide the other layer over the filling, centering it over the bottom layer, and spread with 1 cup of the coffee whipped cream.

Carefully transfer the remaining cake layer onto a plate so that it is top up, and cut it horizontally into two even layers. Use the bottom of the tart or springform pan to lift the top layer and set it aside. Use the pastry brush to lightly brush the top of each layer with the coffee syrup. Carefully slide the bottom layer onto the cake and spread with the remaining ganache. Carefully slide the remaining layer over the filling. Spread the remaining coffee whipped cream over the top of the cake. You will have a four-layer cake with alternating layers of ganache and coffee whipped cream. Leaving a whipped cream border of about 1½ in (4 cm) around the top of the cake, arrange the chocolate shards in the center of the cake. Remove the paper strips and discard them.

Use a large, sharp knife to cut the cake, carefully wiping it clean after each slice.

The cake can be covered carefully and refrigerated for up to 2 days.

the new brooklyn chocolate blackout cake

When I was a kid, my family spent summers at my grandfather's house in Brooklyn, New York. My mom was a great baker but never baked in the summer. She had Ebinger's. It was just a few blocks away and sold blueberry crumb pies, lemon meringue tarts, and Parker House rolls that were just as good as homemade. For company dinners, there was Ebinger's special chocolate blackout cake. It had three layers of chocolate cake and a creamy chocolate filling, and was covered with thick fudge frosting and chocolate cake crumbs. Ebinger's is long gone, but the cake recipe has appeared now and again in publications. My "new and improved" version has the same puddinglike filling, but it is slightly thicker and stays firmly on the cake layers. This dark chocolate cake also has the same tender texture, but is easy to mix and does not require beating the egg yolks and whites separately. The best thing is that you never have to wait for company dinners to enjoy this cake. It is yours for the baking.

❄ Mixing time 30 minutes for cake, filling, and frosting

❄ Baking 350° F (180°C/gas mark 4) for about 40 minutes

filling

2	TBSP UNSWEETENED DUTCH-PROCESS COCOA POWDER
1½	CUPS (360 ML) HOT WATER
¾	CUP (150 G) SUGAR
3	OZ (85 G) SEMISWEET (PLAIN) CHOCOLATE, CHOPPED
3	TBSP CORNSTARCH (CORNFLOUR) DISSOLVED IN 2 TBSP WATER
¼	TSP SALT
¼	CUP (55 G) UNSALTED BUTTER, CUT INTO 4 PIECES
1	TSP VANILLA EXTRACT (ESSENCE)

cake

2	OZ (55 G) UNSWEETENED CHOCOLATE, CHOPPED
½	CUP (45 G) UNSWEETENED DUTCH-PROCESS COCOA POWDER
¾	CUP (180 ML) WHOLE MILK
2	CUPS (225 G) CAKE (SOFT-WHEAT) FLOUR
1	TSP BAKING POWDER
1	TSP BAKING SODA (BICARBONATE OF SODA)
1	TSP SALT
1	CUP (225 G) UNSALTED BUTTER, AT ROOM TEMPERATURE
2	CUPS (400 G) SUGAR
4	LARGE EGGS
2	TSP VANILLA EXTRACT (ESSENCE)

frosting

12	OZ (340 G) SEMISWEET (PLAIN) CHOCOLATE, CHOPPED
¾	CUP (170 G) UNSALTED BUTTER, AT ROOM TEMPERATURE
½	CUP (120 ML) LUKEWARM WATER, 88°F TO 90°F (31°C TO 32°C)
1	TBSP LIGHT CORN (GOLDEN) SYRUP
2	TSP VANILLA EXTRACT (ESSENCE)

(continued)

To make the filling: In a medium saucepan, heat the cocoa powder, hot water, sugar, and chocolate over low heat. Use a large spoon to stir constantly until the cocoa powder dissolves and the chocolate melts. Add the dissolved cornstarch (corn flour) and the salt to the saucepan. Bring to a boil over medium-high heat and boil gently for 1 minute, stirring constantly, especially where the sides and bottom of the pan meet. Remove the pan from the heat, add the butter and vanilla, and stir until the butter melts. Pour the filling into a bowl and press plastic wrap (cling film) onto the surface to prevent a skin from forming. Chill until the filling thickens, at least 5 hours or up to overnight. It will be the consistency of soft pudding.

Position a rack in the middle of the oven. Preheat the oven to 350°F (180°C/gas mark 4). Butter the bottom and sides of two 9-in (23-cm) round cake pans with sides 1¾ to 2 in (4 to 5 cm) high. Line the bottoms with parchment (baking) paper and butter the paper.

To make the cake: Put the chocolate, cocoa powder, and milk in a heatproof bowl (or the top of a double boiler) and place it over, but not touching, barely simmering water in a saucepan (or the bottom of the double boiler). Stir until the chocolate is melted, the cocoa powder dissolves, and the mixture is smooth. Remove from over the water and set aside to cool to lukewarm.

Sift the flour, baking powder, baking soda (bicarbonate of soda), and salt together into a medium bowl and set aside. In a large bowl, using an electric mixer on medium speed, beat the butter and sugar until lightened to a cream color and smooth, about 2 minutes. Stop the mixer and scrape the sides of the bowl as needed. Add the eggs, two at a time, mixing until each addition is blended into the batter, and adding the vanilla with the last addition. Beat for 1 minute more. On low speed, mix in the cooled chocolate mixture to blend it smoothly. Add the flour mixture, mixing just until the flour is incorporated and the batter looks smooth. Pour the batter into the prepared pans, dividing it evenly.

Bake just until the tops feel firm when lightly touched and a toothpick inserted in the center of each cake comes out clean, about 40 minutes. Cool the cakes in the pans on wire racks for 10 minutes. Use a small, sharp knife to loosen each cake from the sides of the pan, and invert each cake onto a wire rack. Carefully remove the paper and place it loosely on the cake. Let the cake layers cool thoroughly, then discard the paper.

To make the frosting: Put the chocolate and butter in a heatproof bowl (or the top of a double boiler) and place it over, but not touching, barely simmering water in a saucepan (or the bottom of the double boiler). Stir until the chocolate and butter are melted and smooth. Remove from over the water and set aside to cool slightly. Check with your fingertips that the temperature of the lukewarm water feels similar to that of the chocolate. It should be 88°F to 90°F (31°C to 32°C) when measured with an instant-read thermometer. Add the lukewarm water all at once to the chocolate mixture and gently whisk until the frosting is smooth. It will thicken slightly when the water is added. Stir in the corn (golden) syrup and vanilla. Let the frosting sit at room temperature until it cools and thickens slightly, about 30 minutes.

Invert a serving plate on one cake layer and turn the cake so that it is top up. Tuck wax (greaseproof) paper strips 1 in (2.5 cm) or so under the cake all the way around to keep the plate clean. Use a long serrated knife to cut the cake layer horizontally into two even layers. Carefully slip the removable bottom of a tart pan or springform pan between the layers, lift the top layer, and set it aside. Leaving a ½-in (12-mm) plain edge around the top of the cake, use a thin metal spatula to spread about half of the cold filling over the cake. Carefully slide the top cake half over the filling, centering it over the bottom layer, and spread it with the remaining filling. Invert the second layer onto a plate so that it is top up, and cut it horizontally into two even layers. Carefully slide the top layer over the filling. You will have a three-layer cake. The remaining cake will be crumbled and used to cover the frosted cake.

Use the thin metal spatula to cover the top and sides of the cake with a thin layer of the frosting. Refrigerate the cake for 15 minutes to firm the cake and filling. Spread the remaining frosting over the top and sides of the chilled cake. Use your fingers to crumble the remaining cake layer into small crumbs. Sprinkle the crumbs over the top of the cake and press them onto the sides. Use all of the crumbs to make a thick crumb coating. Remove the paper strips and discard them. Use a large, sharp knife to cut the cake.

The cake can be covered and refrigerated up to 2 days. Let it sit at room temperature for about 45 minutes before serving.

chocolate zebra cake

This cake is just plain fun to make, admire, and eat. The name comes from the four thin layers of dark chocolate cake filled with white chocolate cream. Lines of dark chocolate zigzag across the top.

✳ Mixing time 15 minutes for cake, filling, and frosting

✳ Baking 350°F (180°C/gas mark 4) for about 15 minutes

cake

¾ CUP (100 G) UNBLEACHED ALL-PURPOSE (PLAIN) FLOUR

3 TBSP UNSWEETENED DUTCH-PROCESS COCOA POWDER

½ TSP BAKING SODA (BICARBONATE OF SODA)

¼ TSP SALT

3 LARGE EGGS

1 CUP (200 G) GRANULATED SUGAR

1 TSP VANILLA EXTRACT (ESSENCE)

¼ TSP ALMOND EXTRACT (ESSENCE)

¼ CUP (60 ML) HEAVY (DOUBLE) CREAM

filling and frosting

8 OZ (225 G) WHITE CHOCOLATE, CHOPPED

1 CUP (240 ML) COLD HEAVY (DOUBLE) CREAM

2 TBSP POWDERED (ICING) SUGAR

1½ TSP VANILLA EXTRACT (ESSENCE)

¼ TSP ALMOND EXTRACT (ESSENCE)

1 TBSP AMARETTO OR ALMOND-FLAVORED LIQUEUR

3 OZ (85 G) BITTERSWEET OR SEMISWEET (PLAIN) CHOCOLATE, CHOPPED

Position a rack in the middle of the oven. Preheat the oven to 350°F (180°C/gas mark 4). Butter a 15½-by-10½-by-1-in (39-by-26.5-by-2.5-cm) jelly roll (Swiss roll) pan. Line the bottom with parchment (baking) paper and butter the paper.

To make the cake: Sift the flour, cocoa powder, baking soda (bicarbonate of soda), and salt into a medium bowl and set aside. In a large bowl, using an electric mixer on medium speed, beat the eggs and granulated sugar until thickened and lightened to a cream color, about 4 minutes. Stop the mixer and scrape the sides of the bowl as needed. Mix in the vanilla and almond extract (essence). Mix in half of the flour mixture just to incorporate it. Mix in the cream, then the remaining flour mixture, mixing just until the flour is incorporated and the batter looks smooth. Scrape the batter into the prepared pan and gently spread it so that it fills the pan evenly.

Bake until the top feels firm when gently touched and a toothpick inserted in the center comes out clean, about 15 minutes. Run a thin knife around the edges of the cake to loosen it from the pan. Cool the cake in the pan on a wire rack until it is cool to the touch, about 20 minutes. Spread a long sheet of wax (greaseproof) paper on the counter. Invert the cake onto the paper. Carefully peel off the parchment (baking) paper and discard it.

To make the filling and frosting: Put the white chocolate in a heatproof bowl (or the top of a double boiler) and place it over, but not touching, barely simmering water in a saucepan (or the bottom of the double boiler). Stir constantly until the white chocolate is melted and smooth. Scrape into a large bowl and set aside to cool slightly.

(continued)

In a large bowl, using an electric mixer on medium-high speed, beat the cream, powdered (icing) sugar, vanilla, almond extract (essence), and Amaretto until firm peaks form. Whisk about ½ cup (120 ml) of the whipped cream into the melted white chocolate until the white chocolate is blended into the cream. Use a rubber spatula to fold in the remaining whipped cream.

Use a large, sharp knife to cut the cake into four equal rectangles, each measuring about 7½ by 5 in (19 by 12 cm). Use a large spatula to transfer one of the rectangles to a serving plate. Tuck wax (greaseproof) paper strips 1 in (2.5 cm) or so under the cake all the way around to keep the plate clean. Spread about ¾ cup (180 ml) of the white chocolate whipped cream over the cake. Carefully place a cake rectangle on top of the filling and spread with whipped cream. Repeat the layers two more times. Spread the remaining white chocolate whipped cream over the top and sides of the cake.

Put the bittersweet chocolate in a heatproof bowl (or the top of a double boiler) and place it over, but not touching, barely simmering water in a saucepan (or the bottom of the double boiler). Stir constantly until the chocolate is melted and smooth. Spoon the melted chocolate into a medium pastry bag fitted with a small round tip with about a ⅛-in (3-mm) opening. Hold the pastry tip just above one end of the cake and pipe a series of curved, connected zigzagging lines over the top of the cake.

Use a long serrated knife to cut the cake. Or, cover and refrigerate the cake for up to 2 days. If refrigerated overnight, the cake is easier to cut and the flavor mellows as the white chocolate cream flavors the cake.

chocolate layer cake with orange cream cheese frosting and glazed orange peel

Chocolate and orange may be a year-round fruit combination, but in the depths of winter when we often feel deprived of fresh fruit, it is especially welcome. The two chocolate layers for this cake are filled and covered with a cream cheese frosting that is flavored with orange zest and scattered with pieces of sweet, shiny glazed orange peel.

* Mixing time 25 minutes for cake, frosting, and glazed orange peel
* Baking 350°F (180°C/gas mark 4) for about 35 minutes

---

glazed orange peel

2	ORANGES, WASHED
⅓	CUP (75 ML) WATER
¼	CUP (50 G) GRANULATED SUGAR
1	TBSP CIDER VINEGAR

frosting

¾	CUP (170 G) UNSALTED BUTTER, AT ROOM TEMPERATURE
8	OZ (225 G) CREAM CHEESE, AT ROOM TEMPERATURE
1	TBSP GRATED ORANGE ZEST
1	TSP VANILLA EXTRACT (ESSENCE)
4	CUPS (400 G) POWDERED (ICING) SUGAR

TWO 9-IN (23-CM) DEVIL'S FOOD CAKE LAYERS (PAGE 28), BAKED AND COOLED

To make the glazed orange peel: Using a vegetable peeler and a slight sawing motion, remove the rind from the oranges in large strips. Use a small knife to scrape and trim off any white pith on the rind. Cut the rind into matchstick-size strips. Put the strips in a small saucepan, cover with water, and bring to a boil. Pour the orange strips into a strainer and rinse with cold water. In the same saucepan, heat the ⅓ cup water, sugar, and vinegar over medium heat and bring to a simmer, stirring to dissolve the sugar. Add the orange strips and simmer for 10 minutes. Use a slotted spoon to remove the strips from the cooking syrup to a small bowl. Cool thoroughly. Or, leave the strips in the syrup, cover, and refrigerate for up to 1 week. Remove the strips from the syrup before arranging them on the cake.

To make the frosting: In a large bowl, using an electric mixer on low speed, beat the butter, cream cheese, orange zest, and vanilla until smooth and thoroughly blended, about 1 minute. Stop the mixer and scrape the sides of the bowl as needed. Mix in the powdered (icing) sugar until smooth, about 1 minute, then beat on medium speed for 1 minute to lighten the frosting further.

Transfer one of the cake layers to a serving plate. Tuck wax (greaseproof) paper strips 1 in (2.5 cm) or so under the cake all the way around to keep the plate clean. Use a thin metal spatula to spread about 1¼ cups (300 ml) of the frosting over the cake. Carefully slide the remaining cake layer onto the filling, centering it over the bottom layer. Spread the remaining frosting over the top and sides of the cake. Scatter the glazed orange peel over the top of the frosted cake. Remove the paper strips and discard them.

Use a large, sharp knife to cut the cake into slices, carefully wiping it clean after each slice.

The cake can be covered and refrigerated for up to 3 days. Let the cake sit at room temperature for 1 hour before serving to let the frosting soften.

Choices: Omit the glazed orange peel and scatter 2 tsp grated orange zest over the top of the cake. Or, buy chocolate-covered orange peel and arrange pieces over the top of the cake; two pieces crisscrossed over each other look nice.

chocolate toffee crunch cake

At least twenty years ago, I saw a photo in a book of a cake baked in a tube pan and topped with nut-covered toffee. I have no idea what was inside, but the image of that cake with its chunky topping lingered in my mind over all of these years. To reproduce the cake, I made a sponge cake in a tube pan, split it into three layers, doused each layer with Amaretto syrup and spread it with ganache, and decorated the cake with chocolate-covered toffee from my local candy store.

Large pieces of chocolate-covered toffee candy bars, such as Heath bars, can be substituted for the nut-covered toffee. The sponge cake takes only 20 minutes to bake in the tube pan because the center tube helps it bake quickly and evenly. Since ovens differ, be sure to check the cake carefully with a toothpick for doneness.

✺ Mixing time 25 minutes
✺ Baking 350°F (180°C/gas mark 4) for about 20 minutes

---

cake

- ¾ CUP (100 G) CAKE (SOFT-WHEAT) FLOUR
- ¼ CUP (25 G) UNSWEETENED DUTCH-PROCESS COCOA POWDER
- ¼ TSP SALT
- 6 LARGE EGGS, SEPARATED
- 1 CUP (200 G) SUGAR
- ½ TSP INSTANT COFFEE GRANULES
- 1 TSP VANILLA EXTRACT (ESSENCE)
- ½ TSP ALMOND EXTRACT (ESSENCE)
- ½ TSP CREAM OF TARTAR

amaretto syrup

- ½ CUP (120 ML) WATER
- ½ CUP (100 G) SUGAR
- 1 TBSP PLUS 1 TSP AMARETTO OR ALMOND-FLAVORED LIQUEUR

- 2 CUPS (480 ML) GANACHE (PAGE 26), COOLED AND AT SPREADING CONSISTENCY
- 2 CUPS (255 G) CHOCOLATE-AND-NUT-COVERED TOFFEE CANDY, BROKEN INTO PIECES ½ TO 1 IN (12 MM TO 2.5 CM)

Position a rack in the middle of the oven. Preheat the oven to 350°F (180°C/gas mark 4). Butter the bottom, sides, and center tube of a 9½- or 10-in (24- or 25-cm) fixed-bottom tube pan with sides at least 3¾ in (9.5 cm) high. Line the bottom with parchment (baking) paper and butter the paper.

To make the cake: Sift the flour, cocoa powder, and salt into a medium bowl and set aside. In a large bowl, using an electric mixer on medium speed, beat the egg yolks and ½ cup (100 g) of the sugar until thickened and lightened to a cream color, about 3 minutes. Stop the mixer and scrape the sides of the bowl as needed. Mix in the instant coffee, vanilla, and almond extract (essence). Set aside.

(continued)

In a clean large bowl, using an electric mixer on low speed, beat the egg whites and cream of tartar until the whites are foamy and the cream of tartar dissolves. On medium speed, beat the egg whites until they look shiny and smooth and the movement of the beaters forms lines in the mixture. When you stop the mixer and lift the beaters, the beaten whites should cling to them. Slowly beat in the remaining ½ cup (100 g) sugar, 2 tbsp at a time, then beat for 1 minute.

Use a rubber spatula to fold about one-third of the beaten whites into the yolk mixture. Fold in the remaining egg whites. In three additions, sprinkle the flour mixture over the egg mixture, folding in each addition with the rubber spatula and incorporating it into the batter before folding in more flour. Scrape the batter into the prepared pan and use the spatula to gently smooth the top. Bake until the top feels firm when gently touched and a toothpick inserted into the center comes out clean, about 20 minutes.

Let the cake cool in the pan on a wire rack for 15 minutes. Run a thin knife around the sides and center tube to loosen the cake. Invert the cake onto the wire rack and cool thoroughly. Remove and discard the paper.

To make the Amaretto syrup: In a small saucepan, heat the water and sugar over medium heat to dissolve the sugar. Remove the pan from the heat and stir in the Amaretto. Set aside.

Use a large metal spatula to slide the cake onto a serving plate, leaving it bottom up. Tuck wax (greaseproof) paper strips 1 in (2.5 cm) or so under the cake all the way around to keep the plate clean. Use a long serrated knife to cut the cake horizontally into three equal layers. Carefully slip the removable bottom of a tart pan or springform pan under the top layer, lift the layer, and set it aside. Remove the middle layer and set it aside. Use a pastry brush to lightly brush the top of each layer with the Amaretto syrup. Pour ½ cup (120 ml) of the ganache around the center of the bottom layer and use a small spatula to spread it evenly over the cake. Carefully slide the middle layer over the ganache, centering it over the bottom layer, and spread ½ cup (120 ml) of the ganache over the cake. Slide the top layer over the ganache, centering it carefully. Spread the remaining ganache over the top and sides of the cake. Put the pieces of toffee over the top of the cake, pressing them gently into the ganache. Remove the paper strips and discard them.

Serve the cake at room temperature. Use a large serrated knife to cut the cake. If it is difficult to cut through any large pieces of toffee, move them to the side and replace them after the slice is cut.

The cake can be covered and refrigerated for up to 3 days. Bring it to room temperature before serving.

salted caramel and pecan chocolate cake

If this were a cereal box, the banner would read "new taste sensation!" But this is a cake, a really good cake. The chocolate cake layers are filled and covered with caramel sauce that has a small quantity of salt, and the top is heaped with pecans that have been toasted in butter, salt, and sugar. Salt plays its usual role of enhancing flavor while creating a subtle sweet and salty combination.

Making caramel sauce is easy. It is a simple process of melting sugar with some water to help the sugar dissolve, then letting the mixture bubble away until the sugar becomes hot enough to caramelize and reach the desired color. The only way to ruin caramel sauce is to burn it. Also remember that freshly made caramel sauce is very hot, so be careful not to splash any on yourself.

Mixing time 30 minutes for cake, caramel sauce, and roasted nuts

Baking 325°F (165°C/gas mark 3) for 15 minutes for nuts and 350°F (180°C/gas mark 4) for about 45 minutes for cake

caramel sauce

1½ CUPS (360 ML) HEAVY (DOUBLE) CREAM

¾ CUP (180 ML) WATER

2 CUPS (400 G) SUGAR

½ TSP SALT

½ TSP VANILLA EXTRACT (ESSENCE)

toasted salted pecans

2 CUPS (230 G) PECAN HALVES

2 TBSP UNSALTED BUTTER, MELTED

1 TBSP PLUS 1 TSP SUGAR

1 TSP SALT

ONE 10-IN (25-CM) DEVIL'S FOOD CAKE LAYER (PAGE 28), BAKED AND COOLED

1 QT (960 ML) VANILLA ICE CREAM (OPTIONAL)

To make the caramel sauce: Put the cream in a small saucepan and warm it over low heat. Adjust the heat to keep the cream warm while you cook the sugar. Combine the water and sugar in a heavy-bottomed saucepan with at least a 3-qt (2.8-L) capacity. Cover the pan and cook over medium heat until the sugar dissolves, about 5 minutes. Uncover the pan occasionally and use a wet pastry brush to brush down any sugar crystals that have formed on the sides of the pan. Uncover, increase the heat to medium-high, and bring the mixture to a boil. Boil until the mixture turns a dark golden color, tilting the pan slightly to ensure that the sugar cooks evenly, about 10 minutes. Once the caramel begins to change color, it reaches the dark golden stage quickly, so watch it carefully and remove it from the heat immediately when it is ready.

Use a wooden spoon to slowly stir the hot cream into the hot caramelized sugar. The mixture will bubble up vigorously, so be careful. Slowly stir the mixture until the cream and caramel are smoothly combined. Set the sauce aside for 5 minutes to cool. Stir in the salt and vanilla. You will have about 2 cups (480 ml) of caramel sauce. Set the sauce aside to cool until it is thick enough to cling to the cake when spread, about 1½ hours. Or, cool the sauce for about 30 minutes, cover, and refrigerate it for up to 1 week. Warm the sauce over low heat just until it is soft enough to spread on the cake.

(continued)

To make the toasted salted pecans: Preheat the oven to 325°F (165°C/gas mark 3). Line a baking sheet with parchment (baking) paper. In a medium bowl, stir the pecans and melted butter together. Sprinkle the sugar and salt over the nuts, stirring to coat them. Scrape the nuts onto the prepared baking sheet, spreading them in a single layer. Bake for about 15 minutes, stirring once after 8 minutes. Remove from the oven and set aside to cool.

Transfer the cake layer to a serving plate so that it is top up. Tuck wax (greaseproof) paper strips 1 in (2.5 cm) or so under the cake all the way around to keep the plate clean. Use a long serrated knife to cut the cake layer horizontally into two even layers. Carefully slip the removable bottom of a tart pan or a springform pan between the layers, lift the top layer, and set it aside. Pour ¾ cup (180 ml) of the cooled caramel sauce over the center of the cake and spread it evenly. Carefully slide the top half of the cake layer over the caramel filling, centering it over the bottom layer, and spread with ¾ cup (180 ml) of the caramel sauce. Leaving a 1-in (2.5-cm) plain edge around the top of the cake, spoon the pecans onto the cake, mounding them toward the center. Spoon the remaining ½ cup (120 ml) caramel sauce over the nuts. Remove the paper strips and discard them.

Use a large, sharp knife to cut the cake, carefully wiping it clean after cutting each slice. Serve with vanilla ice cream, if desired.

The cake can be covered and stored at room temperature for up to 2 days.

Choices: The chocolate cake could also be baked in a 9-in (23-cm) square pan (see page 28).

ginger-chocolate
cake roll

When I told my friend Carol Witham that I was writing a book about chocolate cakes, she described her chocolate cake roll filled with whipped cream and crystallized ginger. I asked for the recipe, but Carol did a lot more than that. She came to dinner and arrived carrying this gorgeous cake roll. An especially nice characteristic of the cake is the generous quantity of crystallized ginger that gives the roll a sweet and spicy zing.

❋ Mixing time 15 minutes for cake and filling

❋ Baking 325°F (165°C/gas mark 3) for about 20 minutes

sponge cake

⅔ CUP (85 G) CAKE (SOFT-WHEAT) FLOUR

⅓ CUP (30 G) UNSWEETENED DUTCH-PROCESS COCOA POWDER

¼ TSP SALT

6 LARGE EGGS, SEPARATED

1 CUP (200 G) GRANULATED SUGAR

½ TSP INSTANT COFFEE GRANULES

1 TSP VANILLA EXTRACT (ESSENCE)

½ TSP CREAM OF TARTAR

filling

3 CUPS (720 ML) COLD HEAVY (DOUBLE) CREAM

¼ CUP (25 G) POWDERED (ICING) SUGAR

1 TSP GROUND CINNAMON

1½ TSP VANILLA EXTRACT (ESSENCE)

½ CUP (85 G) CRYSTALLIZED GINGER, CUT INTO ¼-IN (6-MM) PIECES

Position a rack in the middle of the oven. Preheat the oven to 325°F (165°C/gas mark 3). Butter a 15½-by-10½-by-1-in (39-by-26.5-by-2.5-cm) jelly roll (Swiss roll) pan. Line the bottom with parchment (baking) paper and butter the paper.

To make the sponge cake: Sift the flour, cocoa powder, and salt into a medium bowl and set aside. In a large bowl, using an electric mixer on medium speed, beat the egg yolks and ½ cup (100 g) of the granulated sugar until thickened and lightened to a cream color, about 3 minutes. Stop the mixer and scrape the sides of the bowl as needed. Mix in the instant coffee and vanilla. Set aside.

In a clean large bowl, using an electric mixer on low speed, beat the egg whites and cream of tartar until the whites are foamy and the cream of tartar dissolves. On medium speed, beat the egg whites until they look shiny and smooth and the movement of the beaters forms lines in the mixture. When you stop the mixer and lift the beaters, the whites should cling to them. Slowly beat in the remaining ½ cup (100 g) granulated sugar, 2 tbsp at a time, then beat for 1 minute.

Use a rubber spatula to fold about one-third of the beaten egg whites into the yolk mixture. Fold in the remaining egg whites. Sprinkle the flour mixture over the egg mixture in three additions, folding in each addition with the rubber spatula and incorporating it into the batter before folding in the next. Scrape the batter into the prepared pan and gently spread it so that it fills the pan evenly.

Bake until the top feels firm when gently touched and a toothpick inserted in the center comes out clean, about 20 minutes. Cool the cake in the pan on a wire rack until cool to the touch, about 25 minutes. The cake should still be slightly warm and soft, so it is easy to roll up. Run a thin knife around the edges of the cake to loosen it from the pan. Spread a long sheet of wax (greaseproof) paper on the counter. Invert the cake onto the wax (greaseproof) paper. Carefully peel off the parchment (baking) paper and discard it. Roll up the cake in the wax (greaseproof) paper and let it cool thoroughly.

To make the filling: In a large bowl, using an electric mixer on medium-high speed, beat the cream, powdered (icing) sugar, cinnamon, and vanilla until firm peaks form.

Spread a long sheet of wax (greaseproof) paper on the counter. Unroll the sponge cake onto it and discard the previously used paper. The long side of the cake should be parallel to the edge of the counter. Use a thin spatula to spread about 2 cups (480 ml) of the whipped cream evenly over the cake. Sprinkle half of the crystallized ginger over the cream. Roll up the cake like a jelly roll (Swiss roll). Use a wide spatula to slide the cake, seam-side down, onto a narrow platter at least 15 in (38 cm) long. Using the thin spatula, spread the remaining whipped cream over the cake, including the ends. Sprinkle the remaining crystallized ginger over the top.

Use a large, sharp knife to cut the cake, carefully wiping it clean after each slice.

The cake can be covered carefully and refrigerated overnight.

chocolate-covered banana cake

Bananas, chocolate, and rum whipped cream are a made-for-each-other chocolate cake combination. They all come together here when bananas and ganache fill the chocolate cake layers and thick slices of chocolate-dipped bananas decorate the whipped cream topping. The bananas for the top of the cake should not be too ripe.

✳ Mixing time 25 minutes for cake, filling, and frosting

✳ Baking 350°F (180°C/gas mark 4) for about 35 minutes

rum syrup

½   **CUP (120 ML) WATER**

¼   **CUP (100 G) GRANULATED SUGAR**

2   **TBSP RUM, PREFERABLY DARK**

rum whipped cream

3   **CUPS (720 ML) COLD HEAVY (DOUBLE) CREAM**

½   **CUP (50 G) POWDERED (ICING) SUGAR**

2   **TBSP RUM, PREFERABLY DARK**

1   **TSP VANILLA EXTRACT (ESSENCE)**

    TWO 9-IN (23-CM) DEVIL'S FOOD CAKE LAYERS (PAGE 28), BAKED AND COOLED

2   **CUPS (480 ML) GANACHE (PAGE 26), COOLED AND AT SPREADING CONSISTENCY**

5   **BANANAS; 3 PEELED AND CUT INTO ¼-IN (6-MM) SLICES, 2 CUT DIAGONALLY INTO 12 SLICES, EACH ¾ IN (2 CM) THICK, FOR DECORATION**

To make the rum syrup: In a small saucepan, heat the water and sugar over medium heat to dissolve the sugar. Remove from the heat and stir in the rum. Set aside.

To make the rum whipped cream: In a large bowl, using an electric mixer on medium-high speed, beat the cream, powdered (icing) sugar, rum, and vanilla until firm peaks form.

Transfer one of the cake layers to a serving plate so that it is top up. Tuck wax (greaseproof) paper strips 1 in (2.5 cm) or so under the cake all the way around to keep the plate clean. Use a long serrated knife to cut the cake layer horizontally into two even layers. Carefully slip the removable bottom of a tart pan or springform pan between the layers, lift the top layer, and set it aside. Use a pastry brush to brush the top of the layer on the plate with rum syrup. Use a small metal spatula to spread ½ cup (120 ml) of the ganache evenly over the cake. Cover the ganache with half of the ¼-in banana slices. Carefully slide the top layer over the bananas, centering it over the bottom layer. Spread 1½ cups (360 ml) of the rum whipped cream over the cake.

Transfer the remaining cake layer onto a plate so that it is top up and cut it horizontally into two even layers. Use the tart pan or springform pan bottom to lift the top layer and set it aside. Brush the top of each layer with the rum syrup. Slide the bottom layer onto the filled cake, centering it. Spread with ½ cup (120 ml) of the ganache and cover with the remaining ¼-in (6-mm) banana slices. Carefully slide the top cake layer over the bananas, centering it. Spread the remaining whipped cream over the top and sides of the cake. You will have a four-layer cake.

Put the remaining 1 cup (240 ml) ganache in a small bowl. Using a fork to hold each ¾-in (2-cm) banana slice, dip it halfway into the ganache. Carefully place it, uncovered-side down, near the top edge of the cake. Continue dipping and placing the bananas (spacing them evenly) on the cake to form a decorative border.

Use a large, sharp knife to cut the cake, carefully wiping it clean after cutting each slice. The cake can be covered carefully and refrigerated overnight.

lemon-coconut white chocolate cake

Yellow cakes with lemon filling and white frosting surrounded by coconut are a proud tradition in the southern United States. Once you make this white chocolate cake with lemon and white chocolate cream cheese frosting, you will want to begin a new tradition.

The juice extracted from a lemon can vary from 1 tbsp to ¼ cup (60 ml), but the average is 2 tbsp. Firmer lemons will usually have less juice than softer ones. Be sure to grate the lemon zest for the frosting before squeezing the juice for the filling.

✳ Mixing time 25 minutes for cake, filling, and frosting

✳ Baking 350°F (180°C/gas mark 4) for about 35 minutes

filling

¼ CUP (30 G) CORNSTARCH (CORNFLOUR)

1 CUP (240 ML) WATER

3 LARGE EGG YOLKS

1½ CUPS (300 G) GRANULATED SUGAR

½ CUP (120 ML) FRESH LEMON JUICE

1 TSP GRATED LEMON ZEST

frosting

6 OZ (170 G) WHITE CHOCOLATE, CHOPPED

½ CUP (115 G) UNSALTED BUTTER, AT ROOM TEMPERATURE

8 OZ (225 G) CREAM CHEESE, AT ROOM TEMPERATURE

2 TSP GRATED LEMON ZEST

1 TSP VANILLA EXTRACT (ESSENCE)

3 CUPS (300 G) POWDERED (ICING) SUGAR

TWO 9-IN (23-CM) WHITE CHOCOLATE CAKE LAYERS MADE WITH 2 TSP GRATED LEMON ZEST (SEE PAGE 30), BAKED AND COOLED

2⅔ CUPS (230 G) SHREDDED SWEETENED COCONUT

To make the filling: In a small bowl, stir the cornstarch (cornflour) and ½ cup (120 ml) of the water together to dissolve. Set aside. In a medium, heavy saucepan, whisk the egg yolks, granulated sugar, lemon juice, and the remaining ½ cup (120 ml) water together. Whisk in the dissolved cornstarch (cornflour). Cook over medium-low heat, stirring occasionally, until the mixture is hot and the sugar dissolves, about 2 minutes. Increase the heat to medium-high and bring to a boil while using a wooden spoon to stir the mixture constantly, about 4 minutes. Adjusting the heat as necessary, continue cooking at a gentle boil for 1 minute. Immediately remove the pan from the heat, strain the filling into a small bowl, and stir in the lemon zest. Press plastic wrap (cling film) onto the surface of the filling, use a toothpick to poke a few holes in the covering to let steam escape, and refrigerate until cold, about 3 hours or up to overnight. The filling thickens further when cold. You will have about 2 cups (480 ml) filling.

To make the frosting: Put the white chocolate in a heat-proof bowl (or the top of a double boiler) and place it over, but not touching, barely simmering water in a saucepan (or the bottom of the double boiler). Stir constantly until the white chocolate is melted and smooth. Remove from the heat and set aside to cool slightly.

In a large bowl, using an electric mixer on low speed, beat the butter, cream cheese, lemon zest, and vanilla until smooth and thoroughly blended, about 1 minute. Stop the mixer and scrape the sides of the bowl as needed. Add the powdered (icing) sugar and mix until smooth, about 1 minute. Mix in the white chocolate, then beat on medium speed for 1 minute to lighten the frosting further.

(continued)

Transfer one cake layer to a serving plate so that it is top up. Tuck wax (greaseproof) paper strips 1 in (2.5 cm) or so under the cake all the way around to keep the plate clean. Use a long serrated knife to cut the cake layer horizontally into two even layers. Carefully slip the removable bottom of a tart pan or springform pan between the layers, lift the top layer, and set it aside. Leaving a ½-in (1.25-cm) plain edge around the top of the cake, spread about ⅔ cup (160 ml) of the lemon filling over the cake. Carefully slide the top layer onto the filling, centering it over the bottom layer, and spread it with ⅔ cup of the lemon filling. Transfer the remaining cake layer onto a plate so that it is top up and cut it horizontally into two even layers. Carefully slide the top layer over the filling, centering it, and spread with the remaining ⅔ cup filling. Slide the remaining cake layer over the filling, centering it carefully. You will have a four-layer cake.

Use a thin metal spatula to spread the frosting thickly over the top and sides of the cake. Press the coconut onto the top and sides of the cake, covering it completely. Remove the paper strips and discard them.

Cover the cake and refrigerate it for at least 2 hours or up to 2 days. Use a large, sharp knife to cut the cake. Serve cold.

deep-dish white chocolate peaches-and-cream cake

Summer in a bowl is what comes to my mind when I serve this cool and creamy white chocolate and peach combination. The thin layers of white chocolate cake, peaches, and white chocolate whipped cream are stacked in a deep glass bowl to show off the gorgeous colors and textures. The cake has a spectacular topping of pieces of white chocolate swirled with peach-colored white chocolate. The peaches do not need to be peeled before cutting into thin slices.

✳ Mixing time 20 minutes for cake and filling

✳ Baking 350°F (180°C/gas mark 4) for about 35 minutes

1½ LB (680 G) RIPE PEACHES

1 TBSP GRANULATED SUGAR

8 OZ (225 G) WHITE CHOCOLATE, CHOPPED

1 CUP (240 ML) COLD HEAVY (DOUBLE) CREAM

2 TBSP POWDERED (ICING) SUGAR, PLUS MORE FOR DUSTING

1 TBSP RUM, PREFERABLY DARK

1 TSP VANILLA EXTRACT (ESSENCE)

ONE 9-IN (23-CM) SQUARE WHITE CHOCOLATE CAKE (PAGE 30), BAKED AND COOLED

12-BY-6-IN (30.5-BY-15-CM) SLAB OF WHITE CHOCOLATE SWIRLED WITH PEACH-COLORED WHITE CHOCOLATE (SEE PAGE 15), BROKEN INTO RANDOM-SIZE PIECES

Have ready a bowl, preferably glass, with a capacity of 2½ to 3 qt (2.4 to 2.8 L).

Halve and pit the peaches, then cut them into slices about ⅛ in (3 mm) thick. Put the peaches in a medium bowl, sprinkle with the granulated sugar, and stir the peaches and sugar together. Let sit for 30 minutes.

Put the white chocolate in a heatproof bowl (or the top of a double boiler) and place it over, but not touching, barely simmering water in a saucepan (or the bottom of the double boiler). Stir until the white chocolate is melted and smooth. Scrape into a medium bowl and cool slightly while you whip the cream.

In a large bowl, using an electric mixer on medium-high speed, beat the cream, 2 tbsp powdered (icing) sugar, rum, and vanilla until firm peaks form. Whisk about 1 cup (240 ml) of the whipped cream into the melted white chocolate. Use a rubber spatula to fold the remaining whipped cream into the white chocolate mixture.

Cut the cake into slices about ⅜ in (1 cm) thick. Line the bottom of the bowl with cake. Cover the cake with a layer of peaches. If any liquid has formed in the bowl holding the peaches, spoon some of it over the peaches. Spread a layer of about 1 cup (240 ml) whipped cream over the peaches. Repeat the layers two more times. Arrange the white chocolate pieces over the top and dust with powdered sugar.

Use a large spoon to dig down through the layers to the bottom of the bowl when scooping out each serving. Serve it cold.

The cake can be covered and refrigerated for up to 2 days.

hazelnut crunch and chocolate cream cake

Crisp texture meets creamy and creamier in this cake. Layers of buttery chocolate-hazelnut pastry are sandwiched together with a smooth, firm chocolate cream filling, then are covered with hazelnut (filbert) whipped cream and crumbs of the same pastry. Once stacked and filled, the three layers of different sizes create an attractive dome shape.

The buttery dough is simply pressed onto a baking sheet (tray)—no rolling is necessary. Use one with two or three rimless sides, and the pastry layers will slide off easily.

✳ Mixing time 20 minutes for pastry, filling, and topping

✳ Baking 350°F (180°C/gas mark 4) for about 20 minutes

pastry

- 1 CUP (130 G) UNBLEACHED ALL-PURPOSE (PLAIN) FLOUR
- ¾ CUP (100 G) CAKE (SOFT-WHEAT) FLOUR
- ¼ CUP (25 G) UNSWEETENED DUTCH-PROCESS COCOA POWDER
- ½ TSP SALT
- ½ CUP (100 G) PACKED LIGHT BROWN SUGAR
- 1 CUP (225 G) COLD UNSALTED BUTTER, CUT INTO 16 PIECES
- ¾ CUP (90 G) FINELY CHOPPED, PEELED AND TOASTED (SEE PAGE 17) HAZELNUTS (FILBERTS)
- 1 TSP VANILLA EXTRACT (ESSENCE)
- 2 TSP COLD WATER

filling

- 4 OZ (115 G) UNSWEETENED CHOCOLATE, CHOPPED
- ⅔ CUP (165 ML) HEAVY (DOUBLE) CREAM
- 1 CUP (225 G) UNSALTED BUTTER, AT ROOM TEMPERATURE
- 1¼ CUPS (250 G) PACKED LIGHT BROWN SUGAR
- 1 TSP VANILLA EXTRACT (ESSENCE)

topping

- 1 CUP (240 ML) COLD HEAVY (DOUBLE) CREAM
- 2 TBSP POWDERED (ICING) SUGAR
- 1 TSP VANILLA EXTRACT (ESSENCE)
- 1 TBSP FRANGELICO LIQUEUR

Position a rack in the middle of the oven. Preheat the oven to 350°F (180°C/gas mark 4). Butter a 14-by-17-in (35.5-by-43-cm) rimless baking sheet (tray). Have ready three parchment (baking) paper or cardboard circles, 9 in (23 cm), 8 in (20 cm), and 6 in (15 cm) in diameter, to use as guides for cutting the baked pastry.

To make the pastry: In a large bowl, using an electric mixer on low speed, mix both flours, the cocoa powder, salt, and brown sugar to blend them. Mix in the butter pieces until they are the size of peas. You will still see loose flour. Mix in the hazelnuts (filberts). With the mixer running, add the vanilla and cold water, mixing just until the dough forms large clumps that hold together. The mixture will look like cookie dough. Drop spoonfuls of the dough over the prepared baking sheet, leaving a ½-in (12-mm) plain edge around the pan. Press the dough into an even layer about ¼ in (6 mm) thick. Bake until the top of the pastry feels firm when lightly touched, about 15 minutes.

Remove the pan from the oven and immediately arrange the three paper circles over the warm pastry. Use a small, sharp knife to cut out the circles, being sure to cut all of the way through the pastry. The warm pastry is soft and becomes crisp when cool. Leave the pastry on the baking sheet to cool completely, about 1½ hours.

To make the filling: Put the chocolate and cream in a heat-proof bowl (or the top of a double boiler) and place it over, but not touching, barely simmering water in a saucepan (or the bottom of the double boiler). Stir constantly until the chocolate is melted and the mixture is smooth. Remove from over the water and set aside to cool to room temperature, about 15 minutes.

In a large bowl, using an electric mixer on medium speed, beat the butter until smooth, about 15 seconds. Beat in the brown sugar and vanilla until the mixture is smoothly blended, about 2 minutes. Add the cooled chocolate mixture and beat for 1 minute more. Stop the mixer and scrape the sides of the bowl to incorporate all of the chocolate. If the chocolate cream is too soft to spread easily, refrigerate it for 10 to 15 minutes to firm it slightly.

Use a small, sharp knife to cut the scraps of pastry away from the three circles. Remove the scraps and leave the circles on the baking sheet. Put the pastry scraps between two sheets of wax (greaseproof) paper, and use a rolling pin to crush them into coarse crumbs. Set aside.

Slide the removable bottom of a tart pan under the 9-in (23-cm) pastry layer and transfer it to a serving plate. It is unlikely that it will break, but if it does, piece the circle together on the plate. The chocolate cream will cover the pieces and hold them together. Tuck wax (greaseproof) paper strips 1 in (2.5 cm) or so under the layer all the way around to keep the plate clean. Use a thin metal spatula to spread 1¼ cups (300 ml) of the chocolate cream filling over the pastry. Use the tart pan bottom to lift the 8-in (20-cm) pastry layer and center it on the filling. Spread with ¾ cup (180 ml) of the chocolate cream. Again using the tart pan bottom, center the 6-in (15-cm) pastry layer on the filling. Spread with a thin layer of the filling, and then spread any remaining filling over the sides of the cake. Refrigerate the cake to firm the filling while you whip the cream.

To make the topping: In a large bowl, using an electric mixer on medium-high speed, beat the cream, powdered (icing) sugar, vanilla, and liqueur until firm peaks form.

Use a thin metal spatula to spread the whipped cream over the top and sides of the cake. Sprinkle the reserved crumbs over the cake. You may not use all of the crumbs; the remaining crumbs can be sprinkled over ice cream. Remove the paper strips and discard them. Cover the cake and refrigerate it for at least 4 hours or up to overnight.

Let the cake sit at room temperature for 15 minutes before serving, to soften the chocolate filling slightly. Use a large serrated knife to cut the cake into slices.

coffee-toffee ice cream sandwich cake

MAKES 12 SERVINGS

This ice cream sandwich is party size for serving a crowd. The two thin layers of cake, resembling a fudge brownie, are filled with ice cream and covered with chocolate toffee bits. Make the cake as long as two weeks ahead, and you have a dessert ready for a summer barbecue or pool party.

❊ Mixing time 10 minutes

❊ Baking 325°F (165°C/gas mark 3) for about 16 minutes

cake

½ CUP (115 G) UNSALTED BUTTER, CUT INTO 8 PIECES

2 OZ (55 G) SEMISWEET (PLAIN) CHOCOLATE, CHOPPED

3 OZ (85 G) UNSWEETENED CHOCOLATE, CHOPPED

2 LARGE EGGS

1 CUP (200 G) SUGAR

¼ TSP SALT

1 TSP VANILLA EXTRACT (ESSENCE)

⅔ CUP (45 G) UNBLEACHED ALL-PURPOSE (PLAIN) FLOUR

3 PT (1.4 L) COFFEE ICE CREAM, SOFTENED JUST UNTIL EASY TO SPREAD

topping

2 OZ (55 G) SEMISWEET (PLAIN) CHOCOLATE

¾ CUP (130 G) MILK CHOCOLATE TOFFEE BITS

Position a rack in the middle of the oven. Preheat the oven to 325°F (165°C/gas mark 3). Butter the bottoms and sides of two 9-in (23-cm) round cake pans with sides 1¾ to 2 in (4.5 to 5 cm) high. Line the bottoms with parchment (baking) paper and butter the paper.

To make the cake: Put the butter and both chocolates in a heatproof bowl (or the top of a double boiler) and place it over, but not touching, barely simmering water in a saucepan (or the bottom of the double boiler). Stir until the butter and chocolates are melted and smooth. Remove from over the water and set aside to cool slightly.

In a large bowl, whisk the eggs, sugar, and salt until thoroughly blended. Whisk in the warm chocolate mixture and the vanilla until smoothly blended. Add the flour and whisk until it is incorporated and no white specks remain. Divide the batter evenly between the prepared pans and smooth the tops.

Bake until a toothpick inserted in the center comes out with a few moist crumbs clinging to it, about 16 minutes. Cool the cakes in their pans on wire racks for about 1 hour.

Use a small, sharp knife to loosen each cake from the sides of the pan, and invert each cake onto a wire rack. Carefully remove the paper and discard. Place the bottom of a springform pan on one of the layers and turn the cake so that it is top up on the springform bottom. Replace the sides on the springform pan; the pan will serve as a mold to hold the cake and ice cream. Spread the ice cream evenly over the cake. Carefully slide the remaining layer onto the ice cream. Wrap the cake with heavy aluminum foil and freeze until firm, about 1 hour.

To make the topping: Put the chocolate in a heatproof bowl (or the top of a double boiler) and place it over, but not touching, barely simmering water in a saucepan (or the bottom of the double boiler). Stir until the chocolate is melted and smooth. Remove from over the water and set aside to cool slightly.

Remove the cake from the freezer and unwrap. Drizzle the melted chocolate over the top of the cake. Immediately sprinkle ½ cup (85 g) of the toffee bits over the chocolate, pressing the bits gently to help them stick to the chocolate and the cake. Remove the sides of the springform pan and press the remaining toffee bits onto the exposed ice cream. Wrap tightly and return to the freezer for at least 5 hours or up to 2 weeks.

Use a large, sharp knife to cut wedges of the frozen cake.

party
chocolate
cakes

In our family (and I suspect a lot of others), any celebration is a reason to make chocolate cake. Perhaps this is the Chocolate Yule Log for winter holidays, a chocolate layer "happy" cake for birthdays, a make-ahead Affogato Ice Cream Cake for sophisticated dinner parties, or a tiramisù for a romantic occasion. Each one becomes a sweet, chocolate tradition.

Many of these cakes have simple decorations that reflect their flavors and express the festive notes. Chocolate hearts top the Heart's Desire White Mocha Tiramisù; large fresh strawberries and white chocolate curls decorate the Strawberry, Orange, and White Chocolate Cake; and jam brushed on the interesting dome-shaped Triple Chocolate Zuccotto gives the cake its shine. Any season, any reason—these are cakes that make the party.

affogato ice cream cake

At its most basic, affogato is vanilla ice cream with hot espresso poured over it. At its most extravagant, affogato is this ice cream cake with a chocolate crumb crust filled with scoops of chocolate and vanilla ice cream that are covered with chocolate. At this point, the cake can sit in the freezer for up to a week. At serving time, hot espresso is poured over the slices of frozen cake, softening and melting some of the chocolate coating. Finally, the cake is topped with whipped cream.

☀ Mixing time 15 minutes

☀ Baking 325°F (165°C/gas mark 3) for 6 minutes

chocolate crumb crust

1½ CUPS (150 G) CHOCOLATE WAFER COOKIE CRUMBS

5 TBSP (70 G) UNSALTED BUTTER, MELTED

¾ CUP (130 G) MINIATURE SEMISWEET (PLAIN) CHOCOLATE CHIPS

2 PT (960 ML) CHOCOLATE ICE CREAM, SOFTENED JUST UNTIL EASY TO SCOOP

2 PT (960 ML) VANILLA ICE CREAM, SOFTENED JUST UNTIL EASY TO SCOOP

10 OZ (280 G) SEMISWEET (PLAIN) CHOCOLATE, CHOPPED

3 TBSP CANOLA OR CORN OIL

1 CUP (240 ML) COLD HEAVY (DOUBLE) CREAM

2 TBSP POWDERED (ICING) SUGAR

1 TSP VANILLA EXTRACT (ESSENCE)

3 CUPS (720 ML) HOT ESPRESSO

To make the crumb crust: Position a rack in the middle of the oven. Preheat the oven to 325°F (165°C/gas mark 3). Butter the bottom and sides of a 9-in (23-cm) springform pan.

In a medium bowl, stir the cookie crumbs and melted butter together to evenly moisten the crumbs. Mix in the chocolate chips. Press the crust mixture evenly onto the bottom and 1 in (2.5 cm) up the sides of the prepared pan. Bake for 6 minutes. Let the crust cool to room temperature before filling it with ice cream, about 45 minutes.

Using an ice cream scoop, place two concentric circles of alternating scoops of chocolate and vanilla ice cream on the crust. Make a second layer of ice cream scoops, placing chocolate scoops on the bottom layer of vanilla scoops and vanilla on the chocolate. Freeze for about 30 minutes to firm the ice cream.

Put the semisweet (plain) chocolate and oil in a heatproof bowl (or the top of a double boiler) and place it over, but not touching, barely simmering water in a saucepan (or the bottom of the double boiler). Stir until the chocolate is melted and smoothly blended with the oil. Set aside to cool slightly.

Spoon the melted chocolate over the ice cream and return the cake to the freezer to firm the ice cream and chocolate coating, at least 5 hours. Or, cover tightly with plastic wrap (cling film) and heavy aluminum foil and freeze overnight or for up to 1 week.

In a large bowl, using an electric mixer on medium-high speed, beat the cream, powdered (icing) sugar, and vanilla until firm peaks form. Use a large, sharp knife to cut slices of cake. Put each serving in a shallow bowl. Pour about ¼ cup (60 ml) of hot espresso over each slice. Some of the chocolate will melt and the ice cream will soften slightly. Spoon whipped cream over each slice and serve.

fudge-on-fudge raspberry ice cream cake

At our house, there is always room for ice cream. Make it raspberry ice cream on top of a half-baked chocolate cake, frost the top with fudgy ganache, and you have a colorful make-ahead summer dessert for a crowd, a family barbecue, or another of the season's many parties.

❋ Mixing time 20 minutes for cake and ganache

❋ Baking 350°F (180°C/gas mark 4) for about 20 minutes

cake

- 6 OZ (170 G) SEMISWEET (PLAIN) CHOCOLATE, CHOPPED
- 2 OZ (55 G) UNSWEETENED CHOCOLATE, CHOPPED
- ¼ CUP (55 G) UNSALTED BUTTER, AT ROOM TEMPERATURE
- ½ CUP (65 G) UNBLEACHED ALL-PURPOSE (PLAIN) FLOUR
- ¼ TSP BAKING POWDER
- ¼ TSP SALT
- 2 LARGE EGGS
- ⅔ CUP (135 G) SUGAR
- ½ TSP INSTANT COFFEE GRANULES DISSOLVED IN 1 TSP WATER
- 1 TSP VANILLA EXTRACT (ESSENCE)
- 3 PT (1.4 L) RASPBERRY ICE CREAM, SOFTENED JUST UNTIL SPREADABLE
- 2 CUPS (480 ML) GANACHE (PAGE 26), COOLED UNTIL THICKENED BUT POURABLE

Position a rack in the middle of the oven. Preheat the oven to 350°F (180°C/gas mark 4). Remove the bottom from a 9-in (23-cm) springform pan with sides 2¾ in (7 cm) high and wrap it with aluminum foil. Replace the bottom in the pan and butter the lined bottom and the sides of the pan.

To make the cake: Put both chocolates and the butter in a heatproof bowl (or the top of a double boiler) and place it over, but not touching, barely simmering water in a saucepan (or the bottom of the double boiler). Stir until the chocolates and the butter are melted and smooth. Remove from over the water and set aside to cool slightly.

In a small bowl, stir the flour, baking powder, and salt together. Set aside. In a large bowl, using an electric mixer on medium speed, beat the eggs and sugar until fluffy and lightened in color, about 3 minutes. Stop the mixer and scrape the sides of the bowl as needed. Mix in the dissolved coffee and vanilla. On low speed, mix in the chocolate mixture until blended. Stir in the flour mixture just until it is incorporated. Pour the batter into the prepared pan, spreading it evenly.

Bake until the top looks puffed and crusty and a toothpick inserted in the center comes out with thick batter clinging to it, about 20 minutes. Let the cake cool in the pan on a wire rack for about 2 hours.

Use a small, sharp knife to loosen the cake from the sides of the pan. Remove the sides of the pan and invert the cake onto a flat plate. Remove the foil from the bottom of the pan and discard it. Place the springform bottom on the cake and turn the cake so that it is top up. Replace the pan sides. This makes it easier to remove the slices when the cake is cut.

Spread the ice cream evenly over the cake. Pour the ganache over the top, tilting the pan to spread it evenly. Wrap the cake, in its pan, tightly in plastic wrap (cling film) and then in heavy aluminum foil. Freeze overnight or for up to 1 week.

To serve the cake, unwrap it and use a small, sharp knife to loosen the cake from the sides of the pan. Remove the sides and use a large, sharp knife to cut the cake into slices.

Choices: Substitute mocha chip, chocolate chip, coconut, peppermint, dulce de leche, vanilla, or your choice of ice cream.

spicy cranberry and white chocolate cake

MAKES 12 SERVINGS

Black pepper gives this cake a subtle kick. It is a cake of contrasts—the colorful, tart cranberries dot the pale cake drizzled with sweet white chocolate. The cake is a good choice for making ahead and freezing or, since it stores well, for gift giving.

❋ Mixing time 20 minutes

❋ Baking 350°F (180°C/gas mark 4) for about 65 minutes

2¾ CUPS (325 G) CAKE (SOFT-WHEAT) FLOUR

1 TSP BAKING POWDER

½ TSP BAKING SODA (BICARBONATE OF SODA)

½ TSP SALT

2 TSP GROUND CINNAMON

¼ TSP GROUND NUTMEG

1¼ TSP FRESHLY GROUND BLACK PEPPER

3 LARGE EGGS

2 CUPS (400 G) SUGAR

1 CUP (240 ML) CANOLA OR CORN OIL

1 TSP VANILLA EXTRACT (ESSENCE)

1 CUP (225 G) SOUR CREAM

1½ CUPS (170 G) FRESH OR DEFROSTED, FROZEN
UNSWEETENED CRANBERRIES, COARSELY CHOPPED

8 OZ (225 G) WHITE CHOCOLATE; 6 OZ (170 G) COARSELY
CHOPPED, 2 OZ (55 G) CHOPPED

FRESHLY GROUND BLACK PEPPER (OPTIONAL)

Position a rack in the middle of the oven. Preheat the oven to 350°F (180°C/gas mark 4). Butter the bottom, sides, and center tube of a 9½- or 10-in (24- or 25-cm) tube pan with sides at least 3¾ in (9.5 cm) high. Line the bottom with parchment (baking) paper and butter the paper.

Sift the flour, baking powder, baking soda (bicarbonate of soda), salt, cinnamon, nutmeg, and black pepper into a medium bowl. Set aside.

In a large bowl, using an electric mixer on medium speed, beat the eggs and sugar until fluffy, thick, and lightened in color, about 2 minutes. Stop the mixer and scrape the sides of the bowl as needed. On low speed, mix in the oil and vanilla until blended. Mix in the flour mixture just until it is incorporated. Mix in the sour cream until no white streaks remain. Stir in the cranberries and the 6 oz (170 g) coarsely chopped white chocolate. Scrape the batter into the pan.

Bake until a toothpick inserted in the center comes out clean or with just a few crumbs clinging to it, about 65 minutes. Cool the cake in the pan on a wire rack for 15 minutes. Run a thin knife around the sides and center tube to loosen the cake. Invert the cake onto the wire rack. Carefully remove the paper and discard it. Place a wire rack on the bottom of the cake and turn the cake so that it is top up. Cool completely. Transfer the cake to a serving plate.

Put the 2 oz (55 g) white chocolate in a heatproof bowl (or the top of a double boiler) and place it over, but not touching, barely simmering water in a saucepan (or the bottom of the double boiler). Stir constantly until the white chocolate is melted and smooth. Set aside to cool slightly. Use a small spoon to drizzle the melted chocolate over the top of the cake, letting some drizzle down the sides. Serve at room temperature.

The cake can be stored at room temperature for up to 3 days.

strawberry, orange, and white chocolate cake

Think spring, and Mother's Day and graduations and weddings, and big, ripe, sweet red strawberries. That is the time to make these orange and white chocolate cake layers, fill them with strawberry whipped cream, frost them with white chocolate whipped cream, garnish with white chocolate curls and big whole strawberries, and start celebrating.

❋ Mixing time 30 minutes for cake, filling, frosting, and white chocolate curls

❋ Baking 350°F (180°C/gas mark 4) for about 35 minutes

---

2 CUPS (225 G) CHOPPED, HULLED STRAWBERRIES, PLUS 12 HULLED LARGE STRAWBERRIES FOR TOPPING

2 TSP GRANULATED SUGAR

8 OZ (225 G) WHITE CHOCOLATE, CHOPPED

4 CUPS (960 ML) COLD HEAVY (DOUBLE) CREAM

¼ CUP (25 G) POWDERED (ICING) SUGAR

1 TSP GRATED ORANGE ZEST

1 TSP VANILLA EXTRACT (ESSENCE)

TWO 9-IN (23-CM) WHITE CHOCOLATE CAKE LAYERS (PAGE 30), MADE WITH THE 2 TSP ORANGE ZEST, BAKED AND COOLED

2 CUPS (115 G) WHITE CHOCOLATE CURLS (SEE PAGE 15)

In a large bowl, stir the chopped strawberries and granulated sugar together. Let sit for 15 minutes.

Put the white chocolate in a heatproof bowl (or the top of a double boiler) and place it over, but not touching, barely simmering water in a saucepan (or the bottom of the double boiler). Stir constantly until the white chocolate is melted and smooth. Remove from over the water and set aside to cool slightly.

In a large bowl, using an electric mixer on medium-high speed, beat the cream, powdered (icing) sugar, orange zest, and vanilla until firm peaks form. Drain any juice from the reserved chopped strawberries, and use a rubber spatula to fold 4 cups (960 ml) of the whipped cream into the strawberries. Set the remaining whipped cream aside.

Transfer one cake layer to a serving plate so that it is top up. Tuck wax (greaseproof) paper strips 1 in (2.5 cm) or so under the cake all the way around to keep the plate clean. Use a long serrated knife to cut the cake layer horizontally into two even layers. Carefully slip the removable bottom of a tart pan or springform pan between the layers, lift the layer, and set it aside. Leaving a ½-in (12-mm) plain edge around the top of the cake, spread about one-third of the strawberry filling over the cake. Carefully slide the top layer onto the filling, centering it over the bottom layer, and spread it with one-half of the remaining filling. Transfer the second layer to a plate so that it is top up, and cut it horizontally into two even layers. Using the removable bottom of the tart pan or springform pan, lift the top layer and carefully center it over the filling, then spread with the remaining filling. Slide the remaining cake layer on the filling, centering it carefully. Refrigerate the cake while you make the white chocolate whipped cream.

Put the melted white chocolate in a medium bowl. Whisk about 1 cup (240 ml) of the reserved whipped cream into the chocolate. Use a rubber spatula to fold in the remaining whipped cream. Use a thin metal spatula to spread the white chocolate whipped cream over the top and sides of the cake. Leaving about a ¾-in (2-cm) plain edge around the top of the cake, arrange the whole strawberries around the top. Spoon the white chocolate curls into the center of the cake. Remove the paper strips and discard them.

Use a large, sharp knife to cut the cake, carefully wiping it clean after cutting each slice.

The cake can be covered and refrigerated overnight.

happy chocolate cake

Happy Birthday. Happy Anniversary. Happy Graduation. Here is the chocolate cake for all these occasions and more! When the two cake layers are filled and frosted with buttercream, they are ready for the candles and decorations. Quick decorating ideas include piping frosting swirls onto the top of the cake, using melted chocolate and a plain pastry tip to write a message, pressing nuts onto the sides, cutting out chocolate decorations and pressing them onto the frosting, or spooning chocolate shavings or curls over the cake, as is done here.

❋ Mixing time 15 minutes for cake and frosting

❋ Baking 350°F (180°C/gas mark 4) for about 35 minutes

TWO 9-IN (23-CM) DEVIL'S FOOD CAKE LAYERS (PAGE 28), BAKED AND COOLED

4 CUPS (960 ML) FRESHLY MADE SIMPLE CHOCOLATE BUTTERCREAM (PAGE 25)

2 CUPS (115 G) CHOCOLATE CURLS (PAGE 15)

Transfer one cake layer to a serving plate so that it is top up. Tuck wax (greaseproof) paper strips 1 in (2.5 cm) or so under the cake all the way around to keep the plate clean. Use a thin metal spatula to spread about 1¼ cups (300 ml) of the frosting over the cake. Use the removable bottom of a tart pan or springform pan to slide the remaining cake layer onto the filling, centering it carefully. Scrape ¾ cup (180 ml) of the frosting into a small bowl. Spread the remaining frosting over the top and sides of the cake.

Spoon the reserved ¾ cup frosting into a large pastry bag fitted with a large star tip. Pipe a border of shells around the top of the cake. (To form the shells, hold the pastry tip just above the cake and at about a 60-degree angle to the cake. Pipe a small mound of frosting, then pull the tip forward about ¼ in [6 mm] while reducing the pressure on the bag, and simultaneously reducing the angle of the bag, to form a tail on the shell.) Continue piping the frosting until the border is complete. Spoon the chocolate curls over the center of the cake. Remove the paper strips and discard them.

Use a large, sharp knife to cut the cake, carefully wiping it clean after cutting each slice.

The cake can be covered and refrigerated for up to 3 days. Let it sit at room temperature for 1 hour before serving to let the frosting soften.

raspberry forest cake

This pull-out-all-of-the-stops cake is reason alone to celebrate. The square chocolate cake has a chocolate whipped cream and raspberry filling, and the topping is decorated with chocolate cutouts in the shape of trees.

✳ Mixing time 30 minutes for cake, filling, and chocolate trees

✳ Baking 350°F (180°C/gas mark 4) for about 35 minutes

framboise syrup

¼ **CUP (60 ML) HOT WATER**

2 **TBSP GRANULATED SUGAR**

2 **TBSP FRAMBOISE OR OTHER RASPBERRY LIQUEUR**

filling and topping

4 **OZ (115 G) SEMISWEET (PLAIN) CHOCOLATE, CHOPPED**

1½ **CUPS (360 ML) COLD HEAVY (DOUBLE) CREAM**

⅓ **CUP (35 G) POWDERED (ICING) SUGAR**

3 **TBSP UNSWEETENED DUTCH-PROCESS COCOA POWDER**

½ **TSP INSTANT COFFEE GRANULES**

1 **TSP VANILLA EXTRACT (ESSENCE)**

ONE 9-IN (23-CM) SQUARE DEVIL'S FOOD CAKE LAYER (PAGE 28), BAKED AND COOLED

2 **CUPS (225 G) FRESH RASPBERRIES**

CHOCOLATE TREES (SEE PAGE 13)

To make the framboise syrup: In a small bowl, stir the hot water and granulated sugar together to dissolve the sugar. Remove from the heat and stir in the framboise. Set aside.

To make the filling and topping: Put the chocolate in a heatproof bowl (or the top of a double boiler) and place it over, but not touching, barely simmering water in a saucepan (or the bottom of the double boiler). Stir constantly until the chocolate is melted and smooth. Scrape the melted chocolate into a large bowl.

In another large bowl, using an electric mixer on medium-high speed, beat the cream, powdered (icing) sugar, cocoa powder, instant coffee, and vanilla until firm peaks form.

Whisk about 1 cup (240 ml) of the whipped cream into the melted chocolate to blend it smoothly and lighten the mixture. Fold the remaining whipped cream into the chocolate cream.

Transfer the cake to a serving plate so that it is top up. Tuck wax (greaseproof) paper strips 1 in (2.5 cm) or so under the cake all the way around to keep the plate clean. Use a long serrated knife to cut the cake layer horizontally into two even layers. Carefully slip the removable bottom of a tart pan or springform pan between the layers, lift the top layer, and set it aside. Use a pastry brush to lightly brush the top of both layers with the framboise syrup. Arrange 1½ cups (170 g) of the raspberries evenly over the cake on the plate. Spread about 1½ cups (360 ml) of the chocolate whipped cream over the raspberries. Carefully slide the top layer over the filling, centering it over the bottom layer, and spread the remaining chocolate whipped cream over the top and sides of the cake.

Arrange the remaining ½ cup (55 g) raspberries on top of the cake, then arrange the chocolate trees on the cake. Some can stand up in the chocolate cream, or you can use the raspberries to prop up the trees at an angle. Use a large, sharp knife to cut the cake, carefully wiping it clean after cutting each slice. Make sure that each slice has a chocolate tree.

The cake can be covered and refrigerated overnight.

milk chocolate chip fudge cupcakes

It's party time! Mini cupcakes are great for tea parties, dinner parties, and buffet parties and even wedding cakes. Standard cupcakes are ideal for picnics, birthdays, anniversaries, or kids' parties. These chocolate cupcakes, which can be made in either size, hold a milk chocolate chip surprise and are frosted with ganache. They can be decorated with sprinkles, chocolate hearts, nonpareils, edible flowers, or drizzles or shavings of white chocolate.

❋ Mixing time 15 minutes for cupcakes and ganache

❋ Baking 325°F (165°C/gas mark 3) for about 25 minutes for regular cupcakes and about 20 minutes for mini

---

1	CUP (130 G) UNBLEACHED ALL-PURPOSE (PLAIN) FLOUR
¼	CUP (25 G) UNSWEETENED DUTCH-PROCESS COCOA POWDER
½	TSP BAKING SODA (BICARBONATE OF SODA)
¼	TSP SALT
¼	CUP (55 G) UNSALTED BUTTER, AT ROOM TEMPERATURE
1	CUP (200 G) SUGAR
2	LARGE EGGS
1	TSP VANILLA EXTRACT (ESSENCE)
1	TSP INSTANT COFFEE GRANULES, DISSOLVED IN 2 TSP WATER
⅔	CUP (165 ML) BUTTERMILK
1	CUP (170 G) MILK CHOCOLATE CHIPS
2	CUPS (480 ML) GANACHE (PAGE 26), COOLED AND AT SPREADING CONSISTENCY

Position a rack in the middle of the oven. Preheat the oven to 325°F (165°C/gas mark 3). Line 16 regular muffin cups with paper liners and fill any empty cups with paper liners. Or, line 60 mini muffin cups with paper liners.

Sift the flour, cocoa powder, baking soda (bicarbonate of soda), and salt into a medium bowl and set aside. In a large bowl, using an electric mixer on medium speed, beat the butter and sugar until smoothly blended and lightened in color, about 1 minute. Stop the mixer and scrape the sides of the bowl as needed. Add the eggs one at a time, beating until each is blended into the batter and the batter looks creamy, about 1 minute. Mix in the vanilla and dissolved coffee. On low speed, add half of the flour mixture, mixing just to incorporate it. Mix in the buttermilk to blend it. Mix in the remaining flour mixture until it is incorporated and the batter looks smooth. Mix in the milk chocolate chips.

For regular cupcakes, fill each paper liner with a scant ¼ cup (60 ml) or about 3½ tbsp of batter (an ice cream scoop works well) or to about ½ in (12 mm) below the top of the liner. For mini cupcakes, use 2 tsp (one to hold the batter, the other to push it) to fill each paper liner with a rounded teaspoon of batter, or to about ¼ in (6 mm) below the top of the liner. Bake just until the tops feel firm and a toothpick inserted in the center comes out clean, about 25 minutes for regular and 20 minutes for mini. Cool the cupcakes in the pan on a wire rack for 10 minutes. Remove the cupcakes from the pan onto the wire rack and let cool completely.

Use a small spatula to spread the ganache over the top of each cupcake, mounding it slightly in the center. Serve at room temperature.

The cupcakes can be covered and refrigerated for up to 3 days. Bring them to room temperature for about 45 minutes before serving.

triple chocolate zuccotto

Zuccotto is a dome-shaped cake that imitates the elongated domes of Italian cathedrals. When composed of a white chocolate cake that holds both a milk chocolate and hazelnut (filbert) cream filling and a dark chocolate whipped cream filling, it is a zuccotto epiphany.

The shape of the bowl used for the mold determines the final shape of the cake. Deep mixing bowls that the English call "pudding basins" work well, but any round-bottomed bowl will produce a pleasing shape. A cake that has been baked a day ahead is easier to cut and handle.

✳ Mixing time 20 minutes for cake, syrup, and filling

✳ Baking 350°F (180°C/gas mark 4) for about 35 minutes

---

hazelnut (filbert) syrup

2   TBSP HOT WATER

1   TBSP GRANULATED SUGAR

2   TBSP FRANGELICO LIQUEUR OR ALMOND-FLAVORED LIQUEUR

ONE 9-IN (23-CM) SQUARE WHITE CHOCOLATE CAKE LAYER (PAGE 30), BAKED AND COOLED

filling

4   OZ (115 G) BITTERSWEET CHOCOLATE, CHOPPED

2   CUPS (480 ML) COLD HEAVY (DOUBLE) CREAM

¼   CUP (25 G) POWDERED (ICING) SUGAR

2   TSP VANILLA EXTRACT (ESSENCE)

4   OZ (115 G) MILK CHOCOLATE, FINELY CHOPPED

½   CUP (60 G) TOASTED, PEELED HAZELNUTS (FILBERTS) (SEE PAGE 17), COARSELY CHOPPED, PLUS ¼ CUP (30 G) FOR SPRINKLING

¼   CUP (70 G) APRICOT JAM

Line a round bowl with a 1¾- to 2-qt (1.6- to 2-L) capacity with plastic wrap (cling film), letting the edges extend over the sides of the bowl.

To make the syrup: In a small bowl, stir the hot water, sugar, and liqueur together until the sugar dissolves. Set aside.

Trim a thin slice from one end of the cake and discard it or save it for eating. Use a large knife to cut six slices about ⅜ in (1 cm) thick. You will have six long, thin rectangles of cake. From one rectangle, cut a piece that will fit the bottom of the bowl and place it in the bowl. Cut each of the remaining rectangles in half on a diagonal to make two elongated triangular pieces. Cut each piece to fit the depth of the bowl, trimming it from the narrow pointed end. Save the cake scraps. Arrange the trimmed pieces, narrow-end down, around the inside of the bowl. The edges of the pieces should touch or overlap slightly, and the inside of the bowl should be completely covered with cake. You will use about ten of the trimmed triangles, depending on the circumference of the bowl. If you need more slices, cut them from the remaining cake. You will have some leftover cake for another use. Use a pastry brush to brush the syrup over the cake lining the bowl.

To make the filling: Put the bittersweet chocolate in a heatproof bowl (or the top of a double boiler) and place it over, but not touching, barely simmering water in a saucepan (or the bottom of the double boiler). Stir until the chocolate is melted and smooth. Scrape into a medium bowl and set aside to cool slightly.

In a large bowl, using an electric mixer on medium-high speed, beat the cream, powdered (icing) sugar, and vanilla until firm peaks form. Put 2 cups (480 ml) of the whipped cream in a small bowl and set aside. Use a rubber spatula to fold the chopped milk chocolate and the ½ cup (60 g) hazelnuts (filberts) into the whipped cream remaining in the large bowl. Spread the chocolate-hazelnut whipped cream over the cake lining the bowl. It will cling to the cake and form a layer about 1 in (2.5 cm) thick.

Whisk about ½ cup (120 ml) of the reserved whipped cream into the melted chocolate until the chocolate is blended into the cream. Use the rubber spatula to fold in the remaining whipped cream. Scrape the chocolate whipped cream into the cavity left in the center of the cake. Smooth the top and cover it with the cake scraps. This will become the bottom of the zuccotto.

Cover and refrigerate the cake for at least 4 hours or up to overnight. The filling will firm when the zuccotto is cold. To serve, place a platter on the bowl and invert the cake onto the platter. Release the cake by lifting off the bowl while pulling down gently on the edges of the plastic wrap (cling film). Discard the plastic wrap (cling film).

In a small pan over low heat, warm the apricot jam to melt it. Use a pastry brush to brush the jam over the outside of the zuccotto. Sprinkle with the ¼ cup (30 g) hazelnuts. Use a large knife to cut the zuccotto into wedges and serve.

For the best presentation, the zuccotto should be served soon after it is unmolded. The cake is fine to eat the second day after it has been cut, but will probably not hold its shape.

heart's desire white mocha tiramisù

This is one sexy dessert. Think of that famous scene in the film *Tom Jones*. Then face a friend, a good friend, and dig your spoons into the bowl. You will go through chocolate hearts, multiple layers of coffee-drenched white chocolate cake, dark and white chocolate, and mascarpone cream. You will probably want to lick the spoon.

Mascarpone is a rich, sweet cream cheese usually sold in 8-oz (225-g) containers. It can be found in many supermarkets, Italian groceries, and specialty food shops. Some national brands of mascarpone are quite firm and will need to be whipped with the cream. Some regional brands are soft and creamy and can be folded into the whipped cream. The soft type is preferable.

* Mixing time 25 minutes for cake, mascarpone cream, and chocolate hearts
* Baking 350°F (180°C/gas mark 4) for about 40 minutes

---

coffee syrup

¾ CUP (180 ML) ESPRESSO OR STRONG COFFEE

2 TSP SUGAR

4 OZ (115 G) BITTERSWEET CHOCOLATE, CHOPPED

4 OZ (115 G) WHITE CHOCOLATE, CHOPPED

mascarpone cream

1½ CUPS (360 ML) HEAVY (DOUBLE) CREAM

1 LB (455 G) MASCARPONE

¼ CUP (60 ML) KAHLUA OR OTHER COFFEE-FLAVORED LIQUEUR

2 TBSP SUGAR

2 TSP VANILLA EXTRACT (ESSENCE)

ONE 10-IN (25-CM) WHITE CHOCOLATE CAKE LAYER (PAGE 30), BAKED AND COOLED

12 WHITE AND DARK CHOCOLATE HEARTS (SEE PAGE 13)

Have ready a 2-qt (2-L) serving bowl, preferably glass.

To make the coffee syrup: In a small bowl, stir the coffee and sugar together until the sugar dissolves.

Put the bittersweet chocolate in a heatproof bowl (or the top of a double boiler) and place it over, but not touching, barely simmering water in a saucepan (or the bottom of the double boiler). Stir until the chocolate is melted and smooth. Set aside to cool slightly. Use a clean bowl to melt the white chocolate over, but not touching, the barely simmering water. Set aside to cool slightly.

To make the mascarpone cream: If the mascarpone is firm, in a large bowl, using an electric mixer on medium-high speed, beat the cream, mascarpone, Kahlua, sugar, and vanilla until soft peaks form. If the mascarpone is soft (about the texture of mayonnaise), in a large bowl, using an electric mixer on medium-high speed, beat the cream, Kahlua, sugar, and vanilla until soft peaks form. Use a rubber spatula to fold the mascarpone into the whipped cream.

Use a long serrated knife to cut the cake layer horizontally into three even layers. Carefully slip the removable bottom of a tart pan or springform pan beneath the top two layers, lift them from the bottom layer, and set them aside. These two layers will be fitted into the bowl, and it does not matter if they break. Place one of the cake layers in the bottom of the bowl, breaking it to fit the bowl. Drizzle ¼ cup (60 ml) of the coffee syrup evenly over the cake. Spread about one-third of the mascarpone cream over the cake. Drizzle about half of the melted bittersweet chocolate and half of the melted white chocolate over the cream. The cold cream will firm up both chocolates. Repeat, using another layer of cake, ¼ cup (60 ml) syrup, half of the remaining mascarpone cream, and all of the remaining melted semisweet and white chocolates. Slide the remaining cake layer carefully onto the top, drizzle with the remaining syrup and spread with the remaining mascarpone cream. Arrange the chocolate hearts over the top. Cover the cake and refrigerate for at least 4 hours or up to overnight.

To serve, use a large spoon to dig down through the layers and spoon the cake into shallow bowls.

chocolate croquembouche

Chocolate rules this croquembouche. The classic French version (literally "crisp in the mouth") is a pyramid of cream puffs held together by caramel. This rendition fills chocolate cream puffs with caramel whipped cream. Chocolate glaze acts as the "glue" that holds the puffs together, and drizzles of white chocolate top off this fantasy in chocolate. A nice way to serve the dessert is to bring out the whole extravaganza and let everyone help themselves to cream puffs.

❋ Mixing time 25 minutes for pastry, filling, and glaze

❋ Baking 350°F (180°C/gas mark 4) for about 30 minutes

cream puffs

¾ CUP (180 ML) WATER

¼ CUP (60 ML) WHOLE MILK

¼ CUP (55 G) UNSALTED BUTTER, CUT INTO PIECES

2 TBSP GRANULATED SUGAR

¼ TSP SALT

¾ CUP (100 G) PLUS 2 TBSP UNBLEACHED ALL-PURPOSE (PLAIN) FLOUR

2 TBSP UNSWEETENED DUTCH-PROCESS COCOA POWDER, SIFTED

4 LARGE EGGS

chocolate glaze

¼ CUP (60 ML) HEAVY (DOUBLE) CREAM

¼ CUP (55 G) UNSALTED BUTTER, CUT INTO PIECES

2 TBSP CORN (GOLDEN) SYRUP

4 OZ (115 G) BITTERSWEET CHOCOLATE, CHOPPED

1 TSP VANILLA EXTRACT (ESSENCE)

filling

1¼ CUPS (300 ML) COLD HEAVY (DOUBLE) CREAM

¼ CUP (25 G) POWDERED (ICING) SUGAR

1 TSP VANILLA EXTRACT (ESSENCE)

½ CUP (120 ML) CARAMEL SAUCE (PAGE 97), COOLED TO ROOM TEMPERATURE FOR ABOUT 1½ HOURS

1 OZ (30 G) WHITE CHOCOLATE, CHOPPED

Position a rack in the middle of the oven. Preheat the oven to 350°F (180°C/gas mark 4). Line a baking sheet with parchment (baking) paper and butter the paper.

To make the cream puffs: In a medium, heavy saucepan, bring the water, milk, butter, granulated sugar, and salt to a boil over medium-high heat, stirring constantly until the butter melts and the sugar dissolves. Remove from the heat. Add the flour and cocoa powder all at once, stirring vigorously with a wooden spoon until incorporated. Place the saucepan over low heat and stir until the dough forms a ball that pulls away from the sides of the pan, about 20 seconds. Scrape the cream puff dough into a large bowl and cool for 5 minutes. Using an electric mixer on medium speed, beat in the eggs one at time, beating until each egg is blended smoothly into the dough before adding the next.

Drop the batter by heaping teaspoons onto the prepared baking sheet, forming thirty-six mounds about 1½ in (4 cm) in diameter and spacing the mounds 1 in (2.5 cm) apart. Press the top of each mound with a wet finger to smooth any points. Bake until the tops are firm, form small cracks, and are no longer shiny, about 30 minutes. Cool the cream puffs in the pan on a wire rack for 10 minutes. Transfer the cream puffs to a wire rack, and use the tip of a small knife to cut a small slit in the bottom of each cream puff to let steam escape. Cool completely.

To make the glaze: In a medium saucepan, heat the cream, butter, and corn (golden) syrup over low heat until the cream is hot and the butter melts. Do not let the mixture boil. Remove from the heat, add the chocolate, and let it sit in the hot cream mixture for about 30 seconds to soften. Whisk the glaze until it is smooth and all of the chocolate is melted. Stir in the vanilla. Set the glaze aside to cool until it is thick enough to cling to the cream puffs, about 15 minutes.

To make the filling: In a large bowl, using an electric mixer on medium-high speed, beat the cream, powdered (icing) sugar, and vanilla until soft peaks form. Stop the mixer, add the caramel sauce, and beat on low speed until the caramel is blended. Then increase the speed to medium-high and beat until firm peaks form.

Put the white chocolate in a heatproof bowl (or the top of a double boiler) and place it over, but not touching, barely simmering water in a saucepan (or the bottom of the double boiler). Stir until the chocolate is melted and smooth. Remove from over the water and set aside to cool slightly.

Spoon the filling into a pastry bag fitted with a ¼-in (6-mm) plain round tip. Pipe the filling into each puff through the slit in the bottom. Arrange twelve to fourteen puffs in a circle on a serving plate. The puffs should barely touch, and the tops should face slightly outward. Drizzle the glaze lightly over the top of each puff. The glaze will hold the puffs in place. Arrange additional puffs in a smaller circle on top of the first layer of puffs and drizzle with the glaze. Continue making smaller circles of cream puffs, and forming a pyramid or cone shape, until all of the puffs are used. Drizzle the remaining chocolate glaze over the croquembouche. Let the glaze set, about 10 minutes. Use a teaspoon to drizzle the melted white chocolate over the croquembouche.

Use a large spoon and fork to remove the cream puffs to serving plates (three or four per serving) or let guests help themselves. The croquembouche can be covered and refrigerated overnight.

Choices: Since this is a party dessert, more servings may be desired. Double the ingredients for the cream puffs, glaze, and filling, and make one large croquembouche or two of the original size. Coffee-flavored whipped cream or vanilla whipped cream are other options for filling the cream puffs.

chocolate yule log

The French call it *bûche de noël*, the Italians *tronchetto de natale*, and in English it is a *yule log*. No matter what you call it, this is a festive cake. The cake roll is decorated whimsically or realistically to represent a tree log. My log is made from a chocolate sponge cake that is baked in a sheet pan, rolled up, covered with frosting, and decorated with chocolate leaf cutouts and cranberries.

The chocolate leaves can be made up to a month ahead of time and frozen. For a quick finish, the log can be decorated with red and green sprinkles and fresh cranberries, or substitute green jelly spearmint leaves for the chocolate ones. Whatever suits your fancy is appropriate.

❋ Mixing time 30 minutes for cake, frosting, and chocolate leaves

❋ Baking 325°F (165°C/gas mark 3) for about 20 minutes

---

cake

²⁄₃ CUP (85 G) CAKE (SOFT-WHEAT) FLOUR

¹⁄₃ CUP (30 G) UNSWEETENED DUTCH-PROCESS COCOA POWDER

¼ TSP SALT

6 LARGE EGGS, SEPARATED

½ TSP INSTANT COFFEE GRANULES

1 CUP (200 G) SUGAR

1 TSP VANILLA EXTRACT (ESSENCE)

½ TSP CREAM OF TARTAR

coffee syrup

½ CUP (120 ML) HOT STRONG COFFEE

¼ CUP (50 G) SUGAR

4 CUPS (960 ML) FRESHLY MADE SIMPLE CHOCOLATE BUTTERCREAM (PAGE 25)

15 WHITE AND DARK CHOCOLATE LEAVES (SEE PAGE 13)

24 FRESH CRANBERRIES

Position a rack in the middle of the oven. Preheat the oven to 325°F (165°C/gas mark 3). Butter a 15½-by-10½-by-1-in (39-by-26.5-by-2.5-cm) jelly roll (Swiss roll) pan. Line the bottom of the pan with parchment (baking) paper and butter the paper.

To make the cake: Sift the flour, cocoa powder, and salt into a medium bowl and set aside. In a large bowl, using an electric mixer on medium speed, beat the egg yolks, instant coffee, and ½ cup (100 g) of the sugar until thickened and lightened in color, about 3 minutes. Stop the mixer and scrape the sides of the bowl as needed. Mix in the vanilla. Set aside.

In a clean large bowl, with clean beaters, beat the egg whites and cream of tartar on medium speed until the whites are foamy and the cream of tartar dissolves. On high speed, beat until the egg whites look shiny and smooth and the movement of the beaters forms lines in the beaten whites. If you stop the mixer and lift the beaters, the whites should cling to them. Slowly beat in the remaining ½ cup (100 g) sugar, 2 tbsp at a time, then beat for 1 minute.

Use a rubber spatula to fold about one-third of the beaten whites into the yolk mixture. Fold in the remaining egg whites. In three additions, sprinkle the flour mixture over the egg mixture, folding in the flour with the rubber spatula and incorporating it into the batter before adding more flour. Scrape the batter into the prepared pan and gently spread it so that it fills the pan evenly.

Bake until the top feels firm when gently touched and a toothpick inserted in the center comes out clean, about 20 minutes. Let the cake cool in the pan on a wire rack until cool to the touch, about 25 minutes. Run a thin knife around the edges of the cake to loosen it from the pan. Spread a long sheet of wax (greaseproof) paper on the counter. Invert the cake onto the wax (greaseproof) paper. Carefully peel off the parchment (baking) paper and discard it. Roll up the cake in the paper and let it cool thoroughly. The wrapped cake can sit at room temperature overnight.

To make the coffee syrup: In a small bowl, stir the coffee and sugar together to dissolve the sugar. Set aside.

Spread a long sheet of wax (greaseproof) paper on the counter. Unroll the cake onto it, and remove the paper used to wrap the cake. The long side of the cake should be parallel to the edge of the counter. Use a pastry brush to lightly brush the cake with the coffee syrup. Use a thin spatula to spread about 1½ cups (360 ml) of the buttercream evenly over the cake. Roll up the cake like a jelly roll (Swiss roll). Lightly brush the outside with coffee syrup. You may not use all of the syrup. Holding a knife at an angle, cut a slice about 2 in (5 cm) wide from one end of the cake roll. Use a wide spatula to slide the cake, seam-side down, onto a long, narrow platter. Spread about 2 tbsp of the buttercream on top of the roll and about 3 inches (7.5 cm) from one end, then place the cake slice on the buttercream. This slice forms a "knot" on the log. Use a thin metal spatula to spread the remaining buttercream over the cake, including the ends, swirling the frosting to cover the "knot." Wipe off any crumbs that cling to the spatula as you frost the cake. Slide the flat side of the spatula along the length of the log in gentle strokes to form a barklike pattern over the frosting.

Use the thin metal spatula (warm fingers might melt the chocolate) to lift the chocolate leaves and arrange them in random clusters of two, three, or four over the log. Place a cranberry in the center of each cluster, and scatter the remaining cranberries over the cake.

The cake can be covered and refrigerated for up to 2 days. Or, the cake can be frozen for up to 1 month. If freezing the cake, do not decorate it with the chocolate leaves and cranberries. Chill the cake to firm the frosting, then wrap the cake tightly in two layers of plastic wrap (cling film) and freeze it. Defrost the cake in its wrapping, then add the chocolate leaves and cranberries. Let the cake sit at room temperature until the frosting softens to a creamy consistency, about 1 hour.

Choices: Decorations should be whatever strikes your fancy. Options include dark chocolate and white chocolate stars; star-shaped cutouts made with white chocolate tinted with food coloring; red, white, and green sprinkles; colorful seasonal candies; and chocolate shavings.

mail-order sources

Buchanan Hollow Nut Company
6510 Minturn Road
Le Grand, CA 95333
(800) 532-1500
(209) 389-4321 (fax)
www.bhnc.com
Nuts and dried fruit.

King Arthur Flour
PO Box 876
Norwich, VT 05055
(800) 827-6836
(800) 343-3002 (fax)
www.kingarthurflour.com
Equipment and baking ingredients, including unbleached all-purpose (plain) flour, chocolate, dried fruits, and peeled hazelnuts (filberts).

Penzey's Spices
PO Box 924
193000 West Janacek Court
Brookfield, WI 53008-0924
(800) 741-7787
(414) 760-7317 (fax)
www.penzeys.com
Complete selection of extracts (essences) and fresh spices, including high-quality extra fancy Vietnamese cassia cinnamon.

Williams-Sonoma
PO Box 7456
San Francisco, CA 94120
(877) 812-6235
(702) 363-2541 (fax)
www.williams-sonoma.com
Baking equipment and ingredients.

index

O

Oil, 16

Oranges

Chocolate Layer Cake with Orange Cream Cheese Frosting and Glazed Orange Peel, 92–93

Strawberry, Orange, and White Chocolate Cake, 121

Ovens, 18

p

Pans, 18, 52

Pavlova, Chocolate, 75–76

Peaches-and-Cream Cake, Deep-Dish White Chocolate, 107

Peanut Butter and Chocolate Mousse Cake, 57

Pear and Chocolate Crumb Cake, 71–73

Pecans

Salted Caramel and Pecan Chocolate Cake, 97–99

Toasted Salted Pecans, 97–99

toasting, 17

Peppermint Patty Cake, 39

Pound Cake, Chocolate-Swirl Chocolate, 62–63

Pound of Chocolate Cake, 37

Pudding cakes

Chocolate-Apricot Pudding Cake with Chocolate Toffee Sauce, 68–70

Hot Chocolate Pudding Cake, 40

q

Quick cakes

Chocolate-Marzipan Crunch Cake, 45

Chocolate Sheet Cake with Chocolate Truffle Glaze, 44

Hot Chocolate Pudding Cake, 40

Milk Chocolate Chip–Chocolate Loaf, 35

Milk Chocolate Haystack Ice Cream Loaf, 49

Mint Chocolate Crunch Ice Cream Cake, 47

Peppermint Patty Cake, 39

Pound of Chocolate Cake, 37

Raspberries-on-the-Bottom Cake, 41

S'mores Cake, 43

r

Raspberries

Fudge-on-Fudge Raspberry Ice Cream Cake, 117

Raspberries-on-the-Bottom Cake, 41

Raspberry and White Chocolate Truffle Cake, 53

Raspberry Forest Cake, 125

Rum

Chocolate-Covered Banana Cake, 102

Rum Syrup, 102

Rum Whipped Cream, 102